Julie McDonald Zander
and
Nora Zander

This book is dedicated to Edna Fund, whose passion for local history has helped to preserve the past of Lewis County for many future generations. Indeed, without her, this book never would have happened.

Chapters of Life in Centralia

Copyright © 2025 by Julie McDonald Zander and Nora Zander

ISBN 978-0-9768272-8-3

Published by Chapters of Life
Toledo, Washington

www.chaptersoflie.com

Printed in the United States of America

Library of Congress Control Number

Cover design by Kathy Campbell of inkbooksdesign.com

On the Cover: North Tower Street in Centralia, Washington, looking south from the second floor of Terk's Furniture building. The sign is visible on the left of the photo. Businesses on the right include the Peerless Hotel, Gesler McNiven Company Furniture, and Proffitts. Back cover photo shows downtown Centralia during a parade early in the twentieth century.

Contents

Acknowledgments	4
Introduction	5
One: Early Settlers	15
Two: George Washington	33
Three: The Puget Sound War	41
Four: Creation of Centerville	51
Five: A Booming New Century	75
Six: A Centralia Tragedy	131
Seven: Ghost Towns	153
Eight: A College, Depression, and War	167
Nine: Decades of Development	205
Ten: Dawn of a New Millennium	227
Bibliography	243

Acknowledgments

We are grateful to the Lewis County Historical Museum and the dedicated volunteers and employees who have spent decades chronicling and preserving literally thousands of photographs, newspaper clippings, and memorabilia about Lewis County's history, among them Margaret (Shaver) Shields and Margaret Langus. We appreciate the help of Jason Mattson, executive director of the museum, and photo contributions from Brian Mittge and Kerry Serl, authors of *George Washington of Centralia*; Eric Schwartz, executive editor of *The Chronicle* in Centralia; Isaac Harjo; Grace Grant; and Dan Duffy. We also appreciate the help of Linda Kann, who spent hours returning photographs to the files. Thank you also to the proofreaders of this book: Larry Zander, journalist, Christmas tree farmer, husband, and father; Edna Fund, historian; Brian Mittge, journalist and historian; and Jason Mattson, museum director extraordinaire.

Introduction

Long before anyone envisioned a city at the confluence of the Chehalis and Skookumchuck Rivers, at the end of the last ice age, an ice dam holding back a glacial lake ruptured, sweeping icy water across the land into the Columbia River and cutting a gorge on its route to the Pacific Ocean.

In the wake of the Missoula floods, which likely changed the direction of rivers, sprouted a land of lush evergreens and native rhododendrons that fed the Native Americans and wildlife inhabiting the mountains, woods, and prairies. However, an earthquake in 1700 damaged native villages and created a tsunami in the Pacific Ocean.

Living near the Chehalis River among lush greenery were the Upper and Lower Chehalis River Tribes, whose name stems from the native *Chi-ke-lis*, meaning "shifting sands" or "people of the sands." Another tribe calling themselves the Meshall lived at the headwaters in the Cascade Mountains and spoke an Upper Sahaptin language. One of those Upper Chehalis settlements was called Skookum Chuck, which translates to "strong water." Near the confluence of the Chehalis, which the natives called *Nisoolups*, and the Skookumchuck sat *Tuaoton*, which meant "crossing the river." And near present-day Fords Prairie was a village called *Tasunshun*, or "resting place." The *Quiyaisk* or *Kwaiailk* people of the Upper Chehalis Tribe lived in what became Centralia.

Nearby tribes included the *Taidnapam* band of the Cowlitz. Others were the Cayuse, Nez Perce, Quinault, Makah, Quileute, Nisqually, Snohomish, Spokane, and Yakama. The Chehalis spoke a language related to those of the Salish at Puget Sound but traded with tribes east of the Cascades and often communicated using a common language that became known as the Chinook jargon.

Native men built cedar longhouses with the open end facing rivers and creeks, fished for salmon and steelhead in the rivers, and hunted elk, deer, and other wildlife. Women gathered nuts, berries, and edible camas bulbs and wove baskets to carry food and water. The tribe traveled to the coast to dig clams and gather shellfish. They traveled the Chehalis and Cowlitz Rivers in shallow, stone-chiseled canoes or flat-bottom boats, and, when the rivers flooded as they often did, they sought higher ground.

Then early European explorers, referred to as *Wholton* or the "people that floated away" by the Lower Chehalis, sailed past what became Washington state, naming inlets, sounds, and mountain peaks. In 1774, Juan José Pérez Hernández explored the Washington coast and named Mount Olympus, a 7,980-foot peak on the Olympia Peninsula. The following year, Bruno de Heceta spotted the Columbia River, and in 1778, James Cook sailed past Washington for a third time. Nearly a decade later, in 1787, Charles William Barkley discovered the Strait of Juan de Fuca. In 1790, Manuel Quimper named the San Juan Islands, and in 1792, George Vancouver named the Puget Sound and Captain Robert Gray named the Columbia River.

But it was the Corps of Discovery, the cross-country expedition in the early 1800s led by two white men, Captains William Clark and Meriwether Lewis, that changed the lives of Pacific Northwest natives. The Lewis and Clark expedition left St. Louis, Missouri, on May 14, 1804, and arrived at the Pacific Ocean in mid-November 1805. Returning home, the explorers, which included a Shoshone woman from the Lemhi Valley in present-day Idaho named Sacagawea and an enslaved black man named York, camped along the Cowlitz River, which they called the "Cowlitskee," on March 27, 1806.

Next to enter the region were the fur trappers, British and French-Canadians with the North West Company. By 1811, John Jacob Astor had established the North West Fur Company's trading post at Fort George on the Columbia River, the same year David Thompson navigated the length of the mighty river. The British captured the fort in 1812, and, six years later, the United Kingdom and the United States signed the Treaty of 1818 that gave the two nations joint occupation of the Oregon Country, which generations of Native American tribes had considered their homeland. Spain withdrew its claims to the land in the Adams-Onis Treaty signed with the United States in February 1819.

In 1818, eighteen-year-old Simon Bonaparte Plamondon, a Quebec native and employee of the North West Fur Company, canoed up the Columbia River from Astoria and paddled upstream on the Cowlitz River to a landing near present-day Toledo, where he was captured by the Cowlitz Tribe. After several weeks, the chief, Anton Scanewa, released him, but the tall lanky teenager, who had been orphaned at ten when his parents drowned, returned with trade goods. He later married one of the chief's daughters, Cowlitz princess Thas-e-muth, later baptized Veronica, who gave birth to the first of their four children in 1821 or 1822.

Fur trappers explored the region, setting traps, skinning animals, and selling fur pelts for markets in Europe. In 1824, the British-owned Hudson's Bay

Company, which had merged with North West Fur, established Fort Vancouver near the confluence of the Columbia and Willamette Rivers with Chief Factor John McLoughlin in charge. McLoughlin, who has been referred to as the "Father of Oregon," married a Métis woman, Margeurite, the daughter of a Swiss merchant and fur trader and his Cree or Ojibwe wife.

By 1833, the Hudson's Bay Company expanded north to establish Fort Nisqually near the Puget Sound with Plamondon assisting in its construction. Five years later, he helped the company establish its 5,000-acre Cowlitz Farm northeast of present-day Toledo. Cowlitz Farm was the first non-Native settlement in present-day Lewis County. He also built the first brick kiln north of the Columbia River and operated a sawmill in 1848. Altogether, he had four wives and fathered a dozen children before he died at nearly one hundred.

Next, missionaries intent on converting Native Americans to Christianity traveled west. First, Methodist minister Jason Lee arrived in 1834 in the Willamette Valley near present-day Salem, Oregon, where he built a mission school that eventually evolved into Willamette University, the West Coast's oldest university. Then, in 1837, Dr. Marcus Whitman crossed the Rocky Mountains with his wife, Narcissa, along with missionary Henry Spalding and his wife, Eliza. In 1838, the Whitmans established a mission at Waiilatpu in the Cayuse territory near Fort Walla Walla while the Spaldings settled at Lapwai in the Nez Perce country of present-day Idaho.

Farther north, Plamondon is credited with recruiting French-Canadian Catholic missionaries to establish a church on Cowlitz Prairie. Father Francis Norbert Blanchet and Father Modeste Demers in Quebec answered the call, arriving at Fort Vancouver on November 24, 1838. They proceeded north to Cowlitz Prairie, where they established St. Francis Xavier Mission and taught the natives 2,000 years of biblical history and Christianity using a Catholic Ladder carved from shale sticks.

Lewis County continued to come into its own through the mid-nineteenth century. The Cowlitz Trail, a path used by members of the U.S. Exploring Expedition in 1841, allowed for travel between Fort Nisqually and Fort Vancouver. In 1845, John R. Jackson claimed Jackson Prairie in what would become Oregon Territory in 1848. Lewis County was officially named such on December 21, 1845, to honor Meriwether Lewis. At the time, Lewis County stretched north from the Columbia River all the way to present-day British Columbia and from the Pacific Ocean east to the peak of the Cascades. John Jackson hosted the first documented county commissioner meeting in the county, but meetings were also held at Simon Plamondon's cabin and other locations in the county.

As United States settlers claimed more land, indigenous tribes were persuaded to sign treaties to exchange much of their original territory for reservation lands. In 1856, the Quinault Treaty between Washington Territorial Governor Isaac Stevens and coastal tribes of the Qui-nai-elt and Quil-leh-ute Indians was signed, giving southwest Washington to the United States and reservation land to the tribes. A 4,000-acre reservation near Oakville was provided to the Chehalis Tribe in 1864. Between 1855 and 1906, the tribe lost ninety-seven percent of its population, diminishing from approximately 5,000 to 150 people, due largely to disease. In 2020, the recorded population was 767.

NEW YORK PUBLIC LIBRARY, MIRIAM AND IRA D. WALLACH DIVISION OF ART, "INDIAN SUMMER ENCAMPMENT"

An April 1869 drawing of a Northwest Coast Indian summer encampment is above, and below is a drawing of the interior of a Chinook longhouse.

NEW YORK PUBLIC LIBRARY, MIRIAM AND IRA D. WALLACH DIVISION OF ART,
"NORTHWEST COAST INDIANS SEATED INSIDE A DWELLING"

LEWIS COUNTY HISTORICAL MUSEUM P1417

At left is See'-See-Nah', or Secena, the oldest Chehalis tribal member, who was born about 1790 and more than 115 when the photo was taken about 1906. At lower left is an 1800s portrait of John Youckton, a Chehalis native called "Plug Ugly" by local settlers, either because of his flattened head and general appearance, or because he often wore old plug hats sideways. Youckton often begged door to door for food or paddled in his canoe. After he died on September 15, 1901, in a horse and buggy accident, his tribe buried him in the native cemetery on Grand Mound Prairie and referred to him, as his gravestone indicates, as "Skoukuma," meaning "strong." Below are Chehalis native Jim Sanders and his wife, who lived in a village on land later claimed by the Smith family. Jim carried mail to Lincoln Creek.

LEWIS COUNTY HISTORICAL MUSEUM P8473

LEWIS COUNTY HISTORICAL MUSEUM P995

Hazel Pete, born in 1915, wears traditional garb at the 1933 Pioneer Picnic Parade in Centralia. The eighteen-year-old studied at the Institute of American Indian Arts in Santa Fe, New Mexico. She learned to weave baskets early in life and continued the tradition into adulthood, teaching well into her eighties. Below, in June 1971, she's presenting native legends for the Summer Library Program. She earned a bachelor's degree in Education and Native American Studies at The Evergreen State College in Olympia in 1974 and a master's degree in Education in 1978. The Washington State Arts Commission Folk Arts Program designated her a master artist in 1994. In 2001, she received a Washington State Governor's Heritage Award.

LEWIS COUNTY HISTORICAL MUSEUM PC180

LEWIS COUNTY HISTORICAL MUSEUM P9579

Before Europeans colonized their land, the Chehalis people gathered roots and berries for food. At left, Chehalis native Hazel Pete explains to young girls the value of camas, roots of which can be boiled, dried, or eaten raw. The photo below shows Tenes Pete and his wife, Susan, in a horse-drawn carriage in front of a fence, likely on the reservation near Oakville.

LEWIS COUNTY HISTORICAL MUSEUM P2579

LEWIS COUNTY HISTORICAL MUSEUM P2432

The photo at left shows Hyas Pete in the 1930s. He was a Chehalis native who worked for Joseph Borst by cutting down trees and clearing the land. Pictured below are Chehalis natives at an event on the Chehalis Reservation near Oakville on August 8, 1933.

LEWIS COUNTY HISTORICAL MUSEUM P9556

LEWIS COUNTY HISTORICAL MUSEUM P9549

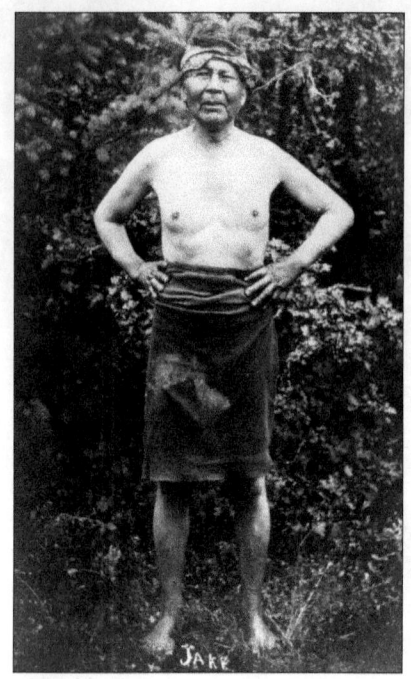

LEWIS COUNTY HISTORICAL MUSEUM P9582   LEWIS COUNTY HISTORICAL MUSEUM P9554

Pictured above are Chehalis native Jake Benn, left, and an unidentified Chehalis woman, circa the 1930s, possibly on the reservation. Jake married Melinda Davis, a master basket weaver. Below, Curtis Dupuis, son of Hazel Pete and Joe Dupuis, teaches foreign students the Chehalis Tribe's legends. He attended college in Muskogee, Oklahoma, and Hollywood, California, before serving with the Green Berets in Vietnam from 1964 to 1967. When he earned a bachelor's degree in business administration from Georgia State University in 1970, he became the first university graduate of the Chehalis Tribe.

LEWIS COUNTY HISTORICAL MUSEUM P9575

One

EARLY SETTLERS

Decades before the founding of Centralia, the Hudson's Bay Company claimed the land north of the Columbia River for Britain and allowed only five families to settle there. The United States and British disputed the boundaries and ownership of Oregon Territory, with the Hudson's Bay Company representing the British. On August 18, 1845, the company reached an agreement with the settlers' provisional government, calling land north of the river the Vancouver district. Then, on December 21, 1845, the provisional government divided the Vancouver district in two, designating the land from the Cowlitz and all the way north to Sitka, Alaska, as the Lewis district to honor explorer Meriwether Lewis. As such, Lewis County is known as the "mother of all counties" because many counties in Washington state today once were within Lewis County's original borders. Finally, in June 1846, the British gave full control of the land south of the 49th parallel to the United States but kept Vancouver Island under English control.

Official creation of the Oregon Territory took place on August 13, 1848. Delegates gathered in Oregon City for the first territorial convention on July 16, 1849, and renamed Vancouver County to Clark County in honor of Captain William Clark who led the Lewis and Clark Expedition to the Northwest in 1805–06. The Donation Land Claim Act on September 27, 1850, spurred even more Americans to travel west to claim 320 acres of free property for a single man and 640 for a couple. But settlers in the north tired of traveling so far to territorial meetings, so twenty-six delegates from Lewis County met at Cowlitz Landing near present-day Toledo on August 29, 1851, and decided to petition Congress to create a separate "Columbia Territory." Then, as more people settled north near Puget Sound, they grew tired of traveling south to the Jackson Courthouse north of Cowlitz Landing to conduct business, so on January 12, 1852, they created Thurston County with Olympia as its county seat. Finally, on March 2, 1853, the U.S. Congress approved creation of Washington Territory.

John R. Jackson, a man born in England in 1804, who later became a naturalized American citizen, built a cabin north of Cowlitz Landing in March 1845, and the first recorded county commissioner meeting took place in his cabin. On a trip to Oregon City in 1848, he met Matilda (Glover) Koontz, a widowed mother of four boys whose husband drowned in the Snake River while the family crossed the Oregon Trail. They quickly married and moved to Jackson's cabin, an ideal location for travelers to rest and enjoy a good meal enroute from Oregon Territory to the Puget Sound. The cabin also served as a post office, store, and courthouse. Jackson, the county's first assessor, justice of the peace, and sheriff, died in 1873. His wife, known for her gracious hospitality, passed away in 1901.

Like Jackson, Colonel Michael T. Simmons, a Kentuckian, crossed the Oregon Trail in 1844 with a party of emigrants but wintered along the Columbia River near present-day Washougal. Among the party was a free black man, George Bush, and his German American wife, Isabella. Because Oregon Territory did not allow black people to settle there, the party stayed north of the Columbia, working at Fort Vancouver during the winter. Then, in early 1845, Simmons led a group of men north along the Cowlitz Trail to the Puget Sound, where they decided to settle with their families. All except George Waunch, a German native who spotted land along the route north where he wanted to stake his claim.

As they returned south to gather their families, Waunch left the party to clear land near the confluence of the Chehalis and Skookumchuck Rivers for a cabin. Simmons established New Market (present-day Tumwater), and Bush settled south of Olympia on a prairie that bears his name. But Waunch, a skilled blacksmith and gunsmith, built his cabin on land that would one day be part of the town of Centerville, and later the city of Centralia, an area known today as Waunch Prairie. He befriended the Upper Chehalis, who called him "Gunsmith."

In 1847, two years after Waunch built his new home, almost three hundred pioneers arrived by wagon train, among them New York natives Sidney S. Ford, his wife, Nancy, and their seven children. They settled northwest of Centralia on what is known today as Ford's Prairie. While traveling west together, their eldest daughter, Harriet Jane, struck up a friendship and perhaps romantic interest in a man in their company, Joseph Borst, but when they settled near the Chehalis River, she opted to marry George Waunch, a man with a cabin already constructed. Theirs was the first wedding in the settlement. Harriet gave birth to a son, George Leonard Jr., in 1848. But when her husband left for California during the Gold Rush, she moved back in with her parents and divorced him in 1851. She married Samuel Henry Williams on May 27, 1852.

That same year, Sidney Ford built a second house on their land and used the second story as a guest house for travelers and visitors. This house was known as the "Skookum House," and the family became well-known for their hospitality. While in Lewis County, Sidney Ford became a judge, county commissioner, and a lieutenant colonel in the militia. He died on October 22, 1866, and his wife, Nancy, passed away on April 8, 1898.

George Waunch returned to Washington Territory in 1852 and worked at Fort Vancouver, then traveled north the following year to establish his homestead claim under the Donation Land Act of 1850, which required people to live four years on the land, construct buildings, and plant and harvest crops. Five years later, on April 18, 1857, in Multnomah County, Oregon, George married Mary L. Hagar, a German immigrant who was twenty-eight years younger. They raised eleven children. It took Waunch until 1867 to officially obtain his land claim of 320 acres. He died on July 7, 1882, at the age of fifty-six. Mary, who married August Sewell and sold off much of their land for chicken ranches, passed away on September 20, 1916, at eighty-four. Harriet Jane, his first wife, died on November 25, 1900, in Grays Harbor County, and their son, George Jr., passed away there a decade later.

Joseph Borst, born on October 15, 1822, in New York, arrived with the Ford family in 1847, settling along the Chehalis River south of the Fords in the park that bears his name. A year after his arrival, he fought in the Cayuse War, a response to the November 29, 1847, killing of missionaries Dr. Marcus Whitman, his wife, Narcissa, and eleven others at Waiilatpu Mission near present-day Walla Walla, Washington. He panned for gold in California and in British Columbia, where he was captured by Native Americans but released. While visiting the Roundtree family's sawmill on the Black River, he met sixteen-year-old Mary Roundtree and promised to build her a large white house if she married him in 1854. He was thirty-three, but she agreed to his proposal, and he kept his promise, constructing a large, two-story white home completed in the early 1860s. It still stands at Fort Borst Park today, along with replicas of a one-room school and pioneer church.

Like the Fords, Elkanah and Laurinda Vianna (Wisdom) Mills crossed the Oregon Trail in 1847, but they stayed with their four children in Oregon City for five years. They were accompanied on the trail by a young New York native named Robert W. Brown, who married Elkanah's fourteen-year-old daughter, Mary Jane Mills, at Jackson Courthouse in 1852. He was twenty-seven. The Mills family traveled with their possessions in small boats up the Willamette, Columbia, and Cowlitz Rivers, disembarked at Cowlitz Landing, and journeyed to present-day Chehalis where they built a home on Mud Mountain southeast of the town. Elkanah Mills, a miller and butcher who with his wife, Laurinda Vianna (Wisdom) Mills, raised eleven children, later lived at Claquato and ran the Astor House Hotel for eight years. Then the Mills family took a homestead on the banks of the Chehalis River in 1867 southwest of Centralia, near where Providence Centralia Hospital is today. The Browns, who raised sixteen children, rented Judge Ford's farm before buying the claim of Peterson Luark in the Skookumchuck area in 1858. Elkanah Mills died in January 1893 at the age of seventy-four, and his wife, Laurinda, passed away seven years later at eighty-two. Robert Brown died in May 1891 at the age of sixty-six, and Mary Jane (Mills) Brown lived to be ninety-two. When she died on May 5, 1930, she was survived by a dozen children, forty-seven grandchildren, fifty-five great-grandchildren, and five great-great-grandchildren.

LEWIS COUNTY HISTORICAL MUSEUM P722

LEWIS COUNTY HISTORICAL MUSEUM P723

Mary (Hagar) Waunch, top left. Her husband, George Waunch, above right, was the first non-native person to settle in present-day Centralia. George was born in Germany in 1812, and immigrated to Missouri in 1837. After crossing the Oregon Trail, he opted to settle near the Chehalis and Skookumchuck Rivers. A skilled blacksmith and gunsmith, he befriended the Upper Chehalis, who called him "Gunsmith." He married his second wife, Mary L. Hagar Waunch, in 1857 in Multnomah County, Oregon, and they raised eleven children. Below is a view of their home. Mary died on September 20, 1916, at eighty-four.

LEWIS COUNTY HISTORICAL MUSEUM P14646

George Waunch married a pioneer settler, Harriet Jane Ford, in 1847. Their wedding was the first in the settlement. In 1848 they had a son, George Leonard Jr., and in 1849, Waunch left Harriet to dig for gold in California, so she divorced him and moved back with her parents. She later married Samuel Henry Williams on May 27, 1852. In the photo circa 1860 at left, she is seated; the young lady beside her is unidentified. Below is George Waunch Sr. with his son, George Waunch Jr., and his daughter, Amelia Waunch, the daughter of George's second wife. Harriet Jane (Ford) Williams died on November 25, 1900, in Grays Harbor County.

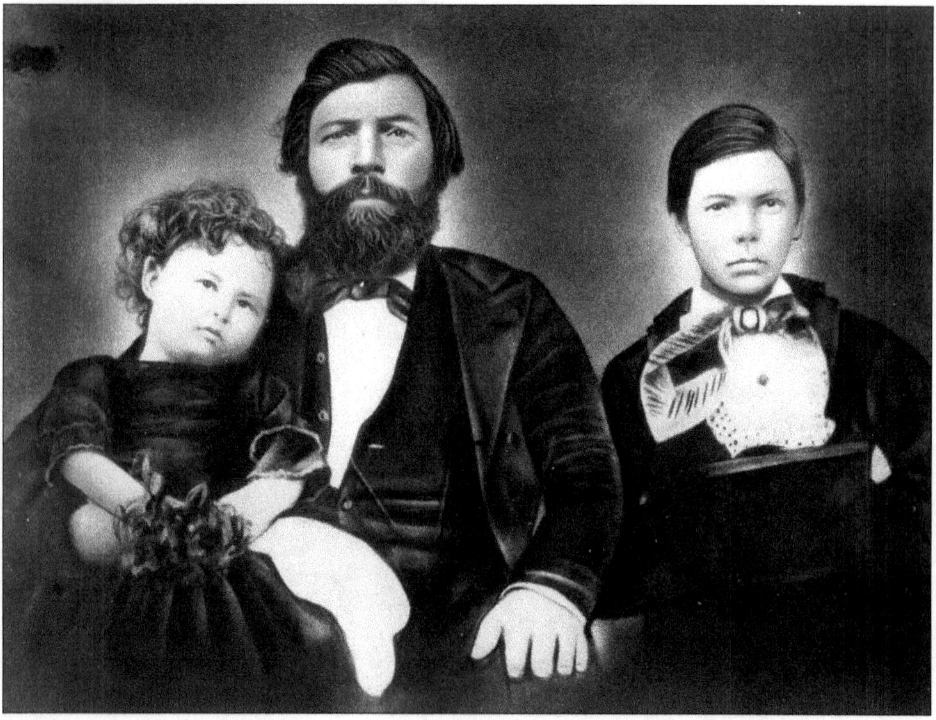

LEWIS COUNTY HISTORICAL MUSEUM P1790

LEWIS COUNTY HISTORICAL MUSEUM P1783

LEWIS COUNTY HISTORICAL MUSEUM P10782

Above is the George Waunch family home built in 1885 at the corner of Eureka and Carson Streets on Waunch Prairie in present-day Centralia. It has a wide porch and an attractive white fence in front. Note the people standing on the balcony. After fire destroyed the home, a second house was built nearby. Below left is Frank Waunch, born in 1870 to George Waunch Sr., and his wife, Jessie (Ford) Waunch, granddaughter of Sidney S. Ford. At lower right, George L. Waunch Jr. and Kate (Wallach) Waunch, with Lottie (Mrs. W.A. Jennings, Flora (Mrs. Chester Sherwood) and Mary (Mrs. J.A. Jennings) circa 1880.

LEWIS COUNTY HISTORICAL MUSEUM P1785

LEWIS COUNTY HISTORICAL MUSEUM P1786

Lewis County Historical Museum P1802

Above, Adolph and Amelia (Waunch) Mauermann settled at Lincoln Creek and raised eight children. Adolph immigrated from Germany, and Amelia, born in 1856, reportedly possessed the strength of her father. At right circa 1930 are Flo (Waunch) Minard, Ed Waunch, Amelia (Waunch) Mauermann, and Frank Waunch, all children of George Sr. Ed, born in 1868, was considered a physically strong man, like his father, and a great horse rider. Below is a photo of the second Waunch home, built after the first was destroyed by fire.

Lewis County Historical Museum P10544

Lewis County Historical Museum P9195

LEWIS COUNTY HISTORICAL MUSEUM P8904

The photo above, taken around 1900, shows a horse-drawn carriage, threshing machine, and steam engine along with eight men, likely some of whom are the Waunch brothers. Below, the Waunch brothers in 1910 at Fishback Farm in Adna. The Waunch brothers threshed grain for local farmers using their steam-powered threshing machine.

LEWIS COUNTY HISTORICAL MUSEUM P8905

LEWIS COUNTY HISTORICAL MUSEUM P1474

Sidney S. Ford Sr. and his wife, Nancy Ford, are seen in a painting above. Sidney Ford built the two-story second home below in 1852 and used the second story as a guest house for travelers and visitors. This house was known as the "Skookum House," and the family became well-known for their hospitality. Photo taken around 1890.

LEWIS COUNTY HISTORICAL MUSEUM P7038

LEWIS COUNTY HISTORICAL MUSEUM P8536

The first house Sidney Ford Sr. built in 1847, above, served as the courthouse for a time. During the Indian Wars, Ford reinforced the windows with bricks, allowing little space for arrows or bullets to pierce the house. The Fords frequently hosted people here on their journeys between the Puget Sound and the Columbia River. Below is a hand-drawn rendition of the residence of Judge Sidney S. Ford, in 1859 by James Gilchrist Swan, who came to Shoalwater Bay (now Willapa Bay) circa 1850. Swan wrote several pamphlets and books and also served as secretary to Washington Territorial Governor Isaac Stevens during the early 1850s. He made this sketch during his travels with Stevens, while negotiating with native tribes.

LEWIS COUNTY HISTORICAL MUSEUM P19220

LEWIS COUNTY HISTORICAL MUSEUM P14199   LEWIS COUNTY HISTORICAL MUSEUM P8191

Above left, a portrait of Joseph Borst circa 1851. He was born on October 15, 1822, in New York. He married sixteen-year-old Mary Roundtree, top right, who led the Grand March at the first Governor's Ball in Washington Territory in 1853 when she was fifteen. They had nine children but only four lived into adulthood. Joseph Borst died on October 29, 1885, at sixty-three, but Mary lived another thirty-five years, until February 18, 1920. The Borst family is pictured below around 1880. From left, Mary Adeline, son Allen Borst, Joseph Borst, daughter Eva Borst McElfresh, and Ada Borst Blackwell.

LEWIS COUNTY HISTORICAL MUSEUM P8193

LEWIS COUNTY HISTORICAL MUSEUM P60

When he proposed to young Mary Roundtree, Joseph Borst promised to build her a large white house, which he completed by the early 1860s. Above at right is a view of the Borst Blockhouse from across the Chehalis River. Below is the house Joseph promised he'd build for his wife. The white, two-and-a-half story house boasted two chimneys, a covered porch, and a garden in the front lawn.

LEWIS COUNTY HISTORICAL MUSEUM P2642

LEWIS COUNTY HISTORICAL MUSEUM P54

Above, from left, are the Borst home, Fort Borst blockhouse, and shed as well as the old ferry crossing location. The blockhouse was built in 1856 to store grain for the military during the Puget Sound War, after which Joseph purchased the blockhouse for him and Mary to stay while building their farmhouse. Below, Mary A. Borst rides in a horse-drawn buggy with a friend, Mrs. Taylor.

LEWIS COUNTY HISTORICAL MUSEUM P4566

LEWIS COUNTY HISTORICAL MUSEUM P2684

The Borst house from another angle shows its close proximity to the confluence of the Chehalis and Skookumchuck Rivers. Below is a photo of the historic Borst Barn taken after the October 12, 1962, Columbus Day windstorm. Joseph Borst built the barn in 1854, around the time he married Mary Adeline.

LEWIS COUNTY HISTORICAL MUSEUM P2695

LEWIS COUNTY HISTORICAL MUSEUM P12932

At left are sisters Eva (Borst) McElfresh and Ada (Borst) Blackwell at an early Pioneer Picnic. Eva married Socrates Scipio McElfresh. They had one child, who died before reaching adulthood. Ada married John Blackwell in 1890. They had no children. In the photo, the women hold a rifle between them, and Eva holds a photo of their mother. At lower left is a portrait of Mary Adeline Borst before 1915. Below is Mary Adeline Borst at seventy-five.

LEWIS COUNTY HISTORICAL MUSEUM P2776

LEWIS COUNTY HISTORICAL MUSEUM P10731

LEWIS COUNTY HISTORICAL MUSEUM P1820   LEWIS COUNTY HISTORICAL MUSEUM P1821

LEWIS COUNTY HISTORICAL MUSEUM P1823

Above are portraits of Laurinda Vianna (Wisdom) Mills and her husband, Elkanah Mills, who was born in Kentucky on December 20, 1818. They raised eleven children. Elkanah, a miller and butcher, died on December 1, 1893, at seventy-four. Laurinda died in 1900 at age eighty-two. At left are three of their four sons, who formed a musical band and entertained at dances and other gatherings. From left are Joseph Moses, William Perry, and Samuel Thurston Mills.

LEWIS COUNTY HISTORICAL MUSEUM P2344

This photo taken during the Southwest Washington Pioneer Picnic on August 17, 1929, in Rochester, Washington, shows Mary Jane (Mills) Brown in the center foreground as the matriarch and "Queen of the Pioneers." Others in the photo are Mr. and Mrs. A.J. Selders from Littlerock, Washington (front row, center), Henry Brown, Art Rowswell, Walter Eshom, Mr. Hemingway, James Fitzgerald, Billie Fitzgerald, Stacey Cooness, Mattie James, Elizabeth Young, Ivar Taume, Ed Pearce, Mr. and Mrs. James McCash, Rev. Miller, A.B. Townsend, Ann Hiaton, an unidentified person, J. Sox Brown, Della Pearce, Ina French, Gus Bannse, Ada Johnson, and Hermann Hoss. Below is a photo taken in 1880 of the Mills homestead built on the banks of the Chehalis River in 1867.

LEWIS COUNTY HISTORICAL MUSEUM P12882

Two

GEORGE WASHINGTON

George Washington, a free Black man who founded the town of Centerville, later renamed Centralia, was arguably the most important figure in the community's early history. The son of an enslaved African man and a British immigrant woman, George was born on August 15, 1817 or 1818, in Virginia. His mother placed him in the care of Virginians James Cochran and his wife, Anna (Calvert) Cochran. At four years old, George moved with his foster parents to Ohio, where they lived until moving to Missouri in 1826. George had no formal education, likely due to his race and a general lack of available schools. Through his travels as a child, he learned many practical skills that came in handy later in his life, such as shooting rifles, tanning hides, and logging. In adulthood, George found ways to work around laws that inhibited the rights of Black people. His white foster father, James, would purchase land and sell it to George, who would then cultivate it. When he was ready to move, George would sell it back to his father who could sell it elsewhere. While this worked for a time, George still faced discriminatory, prejudiced laws that hampered his ability to live and work as a free person.

In the spring of 1850, George and his foster parents decided to head west on the Oregon Trail to seek a better, more equitable and peaceful life. But instead of freedom, when they arrived in Oregon City that fall, they discovered even Oregon Territory enacted laws preventing Black people from settling there. Still, the Cochrans remained in Milwaukie, Oregon, but when George became seriously ill a few months later, they crossed the Columbia River to Fort Vancouver, where military doctors cared for him while his foster parents stayed nearby. After recovering, he and his parents joined Elkanah Mills and his family on the trip north to Cowlitz Landing. In 1851, he set up his parents with a house in present-day Toledo and continued his journey farther north.

In 1852, George decided to make an unofficial claim for land on the southern bank of where the Skookumchuck and Chehalis Rivers met and quickly built a cabin and a farm. Due to its location near the rivers, he ferried travelers across and allowed them to stay the night in his home. In the summer of 1853, George overheard a conversation between two travelers who had stayed at his cabin on their way north and suspected they planned to claim his land for themselves, so he needed to act quickly. Knowing he held no legal rights under Oregon Territory laws because of his race, George asked his parents to claim his land, which they did. The men did try to claim his land, but the Cochrans beat them to it. They lived on the land with George, who took care of them in their old age.

After more than four years of owning and cultivating the land, the Cochrans sold the land to their son in 1858, and he became the official owner. By this time, Lewis County was part of the newly formed Washington Territory, which did not have laws preventing black people from owning or settling land. In fact, James Cochran collected the signatures of 112 pioneers on a petition asking the Oregon Territorial Legislature to give his son full citizenship rights—and it did so on December 17, 1852, with passage of "an act for the benefit of George Washington, a man of color," giving him the rights of settlers despite the color of his skin.

From the time they lived on the farm until 1857, George and James Cochran ferried people across the Chehalis River and cultivated the farm. James had just turned seventy-one when he died on December 26, 1859. Anna (Calvert) Cochran passed away at seventy on February 3, 1861.

Three years later, George bought more land south of his property, and in 1868, he built a new house on his land and donated his old cabin for use as a schoolhouse.

On a trip to Olympia, George met Mary Jane (Cain) Cooness, an African American Jewish woman originally from Louisiana. She eventually ended up in Victoria, British Columbia, where she married a man in 1860 and gave birth to a son, Stacey Cooness Jr., on October 22, 1861. Her husband, however, was abusive, so she left Victoria in the late 1860s and traveled to Olympia where she divorced him in 1869. George and Mary exchanged wedding vows shortly thereafter. He was more than twenty years older than Mary, whose son, Stacey, came to live with them in 1872.

That same year, a railroad built between Kalama and Tacoma crossed through his land. He, Mary, and Stacey began to plan a town, naming it Centerville. By 1875, they officially platted the town and began selling lots. Over the next several decades, the Washingtons donated and leased land for houses, stores, hotels, churches, cemeteries, schools, and a public park (now called George Washington Park).

George and Mary were both known for their hospitality and altruism. They helped the downtrodden get back on their feet, providing work and teaching skills to those who needed it. He asked only for honesty and respect in return. Children and adults alike referred to him affectionately as "Uncle George." His benevolence shone during the economic depression of 1893, when he provided jobs, food, and clothing to townspeople. He remained a calm and steady presence throughout an extremely tumultuous time.

George was also a man of faith, raised on hymns and Bible stories told to him by his mother, Anna Cochran. He often sang hymns, his favorite being "Salem's Bright King."

Mary Jane Washington was only forty-nine when she died on March 5, 1889. She was buried in the family plot of Washington Lawn Cemetery, on land donated by George and Mary. On September 24, 1890, George married Charity Brown, a white widowed mother of three. Although George and Mary had donated land to build the First Baptist Church, more white settlers arrived and decided the black couple were no longer welcome. So, in 1891, George and Charity founded the Second Baptist Church. That same year brought the birth of their only child, a son, George Cleveland Washington, on December 15, 1891. After a half dozen years later, Charity filed for divorce, accusing her husband of being abusive while he contended she aggravated him. Although she sought dismissal of the case in 1896, after they separated, George filed for divorce in 1902 on the grounds of abandonment. Their divorce was granted after twelve years of marriage. Charity died on August 4, 1940, at eighty-five.

During the 1890s, George saw his health slowly deteriorate. He died on August 26, 1905, just a bit more than week after his eighty-eighth birthday. His only biological child, George Cleveland, died the evening of January 3, 1911, when a fire broke out at Vashon College, where he was a student. He helped battled the blaze but succumbed to lung congestion afterward. He had just turned nineteen.

Stacey Cooness, Washington's stepson by Mary Jane Washington, died in 1944 at the age of eighty-three. He was the last living link to George Washington. In Centralia today, Washington is honored on his birthday each year with Founder's Day.

PHOTO COURTESY OF KERRY SERL

LEWIS COUNTY HISTORICAL MUSEUM P9610

A rare photo of young George Washington is above. At top right is Mary Jane Cooness, who married George Washington after escaping from an abusive relationship with her first husband. She had a son from her first marriage, Stacey Cooness Jr. At right is a well-known portrait of George with his dog, Rockwood.

PHOTO COURTESY OF BRIAN MITTGE

LEWIS COUNTY HISTORICAL MUSEUM P1376

Centralia remains the largest city in the United States founded by a Black man. The city is a legacy to the kind and philanthropic son of an enslaved man and a white woman.

LEWIS COUNTY HISTORICAL MUSEUM P4762

LEWIS COUNTY HISTORICAL MUSEUM P8590

Above is the first Centralia First Baptist Church in the winter of 1875. George and Mary Washington donated the land for this church, and George helped with the actual construction of the building. Despite this, when more white settlers arrived, they decided the Black couple were no longer welcome at the church. So, in 1891, George and his second wife, Charity, founded the Second Baptist Church. At left are Stacey Cooness Jr. and Rena (Hickling) Cooness at their wedding on July 9, 1890. Stacey, born on October 22, 1861, lived with his mother and stepfather from a young age. He excelled in school but occasionally played pranks. He was a great singer and whistler and worked for George on the farm. He moved across the street from his parents in 1882. At twenty-eight, he met and fell in love with Mary Victorine "Rena" Hickling in Portland. She was born in Victoria, British Columbia, on December 3, 1871. Rena spent her time mining for gold, boxing, and teaching.

LEWIS COUNTY HISTORICAL MUSEUM P7039

The photo above from 1908 shows George Washington's final house, built in the 1880s. During his time in Centralia, George built four houses for himself and his family. At left is Audrey Cooness in 1909 at age thirteen. Audrey, the only child of Stacey and Rena, was born in August 1896. Rena taught her how to box and, by the age of eight, Audrey could lift heavy items (including her father off the ground) with ease. Also like her mother, Audrey was intelligent and musically gifted.

LEWIS COUNTY HISTORICAL MUSEUM P573

PHOTO COURTESY OF ISAAC HARJO

LEWIS COUNTY HISTORICAL MUSEUM P1068

Above is a late 1890s photo of the Cooness family with guests at their home, built in 1889, in Centralia. From left, Stacey Cooness, Rena Cooness, "Grandpa Hickman," Mr. Green, Mr. Jackson, and Mrs. Jackson. Grandpa Hickman likely refers to Rena's grandfather, Daniel Fredison, who once lived in the South and moved to Centralia in 1896 to live with Rena and Stacey. He died in 1908. The identities of Mr. Green and the Jacksons are unknown. At left is Audrey Cooness at sixteen. Approximately four years later, she contracted tuberculosis. Rena cared for her daughter, but Audrey died of the disease on May 18, 1918, at twenty-one. Rena also contracted tuberculosis and succumbed to the disease on November 24, 1920, at the age of forty-eight.

Three

THE PUGET SOUND WAR

"But I tell you they didn't like it a bit to give in to our government treaty and still they feel and talk to me about the way they were treated by the government. And now they are standing up in their right and it's nothing but just that they are paid for their land."
—Mary Jane (Mills) Brown (1839–1930)

While the Centralia of today is the result of American and European settlers, the land historically belonged to the Confederated Tribes of the Chehalis Reservation. During migration west in the 1800s, the United States government formulated hundreds of treaties across the country to claim indigenous lands and, in return, reserved parcels of land or reservations for the tribes. The Treaty of Medicine Creek, negotiated by Washington Territorial Governor Isaac Stevens in 1854, stipulated that local tribes would relinquish their lands to the United States in return for reservation land, annuities, and fishing rights. The treaty also controlled where the tribes could trade and specified that the president could relocate or consolidate them with other tribes or change their reservation land at his discretion. Chief Leschi of the Nisqually objected to the terms of the treaty, and the Puget Sound War began. Several skirmishes and battles broke out across the region, prompting Stevens to create volunteer militias.

Many local men joined these militias to defend the land they claimed; some notable local surnames include Saunders, Mills, and Roundtree. John Jackson, designated a captain of a local militia company, sent scouting reports to acting Washington Territorial Governor Charles H. Mason (Stevens was busy dealing with treaties on the eastern side of the state).

In early 1855, Stevens attempted to negotiate with the Upper Chehalis and nearby tribes at present-day Cosmopolis, Washington, but no treaty was signed. Judge Sidney Ford and his sons attended this conference, the sons serving as interpreters.

During the war, Ford acted as an Indian agent and lieutenant colonel in the militia. He hosted Chehalis natives on his land but forced them to relinquish all weapons. In exchange, he provided food from the government.

In anticipation of fighting between settlers and native tribes, many communities erected forts and blockhouses for protection. In October 1855, local pioneers began building Fort Henness at Grand Mound, and blockhouses were erected at Claquato (west of Chehalis) and at Cowlitz Landing near present-day Toledo.

Joseph and Mary Borst traveled to Fort Henness with their six-week-old child. Mary's parents, the Roundtrees, also took shelter there. Mary gave birth to their second child at Fort Henness. Joseph, however, returned to his farm and, in early 1856, helped the military erect a blockhouse on his property to store grain. After the war, Borst purchased the blockhouse on his land, and he and his wife stayed there while building their two-story white house nearby. City officials relocated the blockhouse several times over the years until finally moving it to Fort Borst Park in present-day Centralia.

George Washington remained at his cabin during the war but took his parents to Fort Henness.

George Waunch, known as a friend to the Chehalis, stayed at his house during the war. Peterson Luark, another local settler, opposed construction of any forts because he believed they soured relations with the Chehalis.

Initially, the Mills and Browns planned to shelter at Fort Henness, but they chose to stay in a cabin on Ford's property. According to Mary Jane (Mills) Brown, local Chehalis natives asked for weapons to scare off nearby hostile natives. That night, the hostile natives ran to the Fords' house and one of the natives said he would "kill Mr. Ford first." Sidney Ford's son, Tommy, had married a local native, Maskeefe, who understood the words and warned them. The Fords, Mills, and Browns then scared the natives off the property. Other locals heard gunfire and warned those at Fort Henness about what may have happened. The next morning, militiamen from Fort Henness and Fort Borst traveled to the Ford homestead, expecting to find them all dead. As Mary Brown said, they "all would have been killed" if not for Maskeefe.

Mary Jane recorded another local altercation that occurred when her uncle, William Mills, and cousin, Nathaniel Mills, both militia volunteers, were ambushed near Green River. While drinking water from the Green River, Nathaniel was wounded in the neck. His father, William, fired at the native and thought he wounded him based on the way he hopped from sight.

The Puget Sound War ended in 1856 after a final battle in March near present-day Puyallup and the eventual capture of Chief Leschi in November. The chief was tried for murder. One jury split, unable to convict him, but a second returned a guilty verdict. He was hung in 1858, but the Washington Supreme Court exonerated him posthumously in 2004.

PHOTO COURTESY OF *THE CHRONICLE* ARCHIVES

LEWIS COUNTY HISTORICAL MUSEUM P18994

Eva Borst McElfresh, seen above in 1937, shows students Donna Tisdale, Dorothy Rigg, and Evelyn Walking the nightcap she wore as a six-week-old infant when taken to Fort Henness. She was the last surviving person who stayed at the fort during the Puget Sound War. The students helped write Centralia—The First Fifty Years-1845–1900. *At left, a woman adorns the hair of Eva Borst McEfresh while two young girls watch.*

LEWIS COUNTY HISTORICAL MUSEUM P1793

The artwork above depicts Gov. Isaac Stevens, the Fords, and the Chehalis Tribes at Cosmopolis negotiating a treaty. Below is a map and list of people who sought shelter at Fort Henness. On June 14, 1856, a native woman seeking safety from her abusive husband was admitted into the fort. As her husband was leaving, someone inside the fort shot and killed him. Sidney Ford Jr., the judge's son and namesake, prevented potential retribution through negotiation.

LEWIS COUNTY HISTORICAL MUSEUM P11368

LEWIS COUNTY HISTORICAL MUSEUM P20735

LEWIS COUNTY HISTORICAL MUSEUM P1001

This blockhouse built by the military to store grain in 1856 later sat near an eroding bank. When hostilities with the indigenous people eased, Joseph Borst purchased the blockhouse for $500 and lived there with his family while building a two-story white house nearby. City officials later relocated the blockhouse to Riverside Park and then later to the front area of Borst Park. At left, speakers in 1926 mark the role of Fort Henness in sheltering pioneers. Below is a replica made by Charlie James showing what Fort Henness looked like.

LEWIS COUNTY HISTORICAL MUSEUM P5263

LEWIS COUNTY HISTORICAL MUSEUM P8447

Above is a portrait of Dr. James Roundtree, his wife, Emeline Cole (Riddle) Roundtree, and their child Julian Jane, sometime around the Puget Sound War in the mid-1850s. James and Emeline were Mary Adeline Borst's parents. They took shelter at Fort Henness during the war. Their sawmill on the Black River is where Joseph Borst met Mary Roundtree. At left is a portrait of Nisqually Chief Leschi as he appeared in the 1850s.

WIKIMEDIA COMMONS

LIBRARY OF CONGRESS DIGITAL DS-12863 FILE

LEWIS COUNTY HISTORICAL MUSEUM P18944

LEWIS COUNTY HISTORICAL MUSEUM P25000

At left, an unidentified Chehalis man and a young girl who had reportedly been captured during the war are seen in pioneer garb. The Chehalis were peaceful before, during, and after the war. Above, in 1896, George Leschi, a nephew of Nisqually Chief Leschi, wears a feather headdress and holds a bow and arrows. He was the son of Chief Leschi's half-brother, Quiemuth, who was murdered in Olympia on November 19, 1856, after surrendering. Below, a canoe-shaped parade float for the Chehalis Tribe No. 27 Improved Order of Red Men flies the stars and stripes on July 4, 1916, although the "red men" in feathers and blankets were primarily Swiss.

CITY OF CENTRALIA

The photo above was taken while the Borsts were constructing their home in the early 1860s after the Puget Sound War ended. The family lived in the blockhouse while the home was built. Below, a man squats with rifle in hand while a couple stand near the ferry dock.

CITY OF CENTRALIA

CITY OF CENTRALIA

The wood apparatus in the foreground secured the cable for the ferry as it crossed the Chehalis River. A flood in 1880 destroyed the cable and beached the ferry on the bank, and it was never used again, according to the City of Centralia. Below is a family who stopped to look at the blockhouse.

CITY OF CENTRALIA

LEWIS COUNTY HISTORICAL MUSEUM P1354

Members of the Chehalis Tribe participate in the 1932 Pioneer Association's yearly meeting at Fort Borst Park. Among them are Pete Williams, Murphy See-See-Nah, Mike Simmons, Mrs. Pete Williams, Jessie Youckton, Nancy See-See-Nah, Bessy Hoyden, Harriate Pete, Neggue Ben, and Mrs. George Sanders. Below, during the Southwest Washington Pioneer Days Celebration in Centralia on August 3 and 4, 1932, are Native Americans in costume in front of Ezra Meeker's wagon and horses.

LEWIS COUNTY HISTORICAL MUSEUM PC2500

Four

CREATION OF CENTERVILLE

After the Puget Sound War ended, settlers resumed their lives. A new military road ran between Fort Vancouver and Fort Bellingham and crossed the Chehalis River near the Borst home. Ferdinand Chable began a ferry operation at this crossing that ran until 1880 when it was destroyed by a flood and never rebuilt. Stage coach drivers carried mail and sometimes passengers along the military road every day between present-day Longview and Olympia, starting in 1861. That winter, snow covered the ground from October 1861 to April 1862 and the Chehalis River froze. Many livestock and wildlife perished due to the lack of vegetation, but the region still flourished socially and economically. Postmaster Charles Van Wormer opened the Skookumchuck Post Office in 1857 in his home on Fords Prairie, which he operated until early 1863. Throughout the 1860s, the postmaster and location of the post office changed every few years. In 1867, James Tullis became postmaster, and his house served as the first post office within present-day Centralia boundaries.

In 1872, the Northern Pacific extended its rail line from Kalama to the Chehalis River. The following year, the tracks stretched north to Tacoma. A local man, Isaac Wingard, constructed a building in present-day Centralia that served as his home, a store, a hotel, and the post office. Clem Crosby opened a store south of Wingard's and, in 1874, Joseph Young established a hotel kitty corner to Wingard's. Railroad service fully began and soon, dozens of people traveled each day on trains through Lewis County.

George Washington knew the railroad would bring new opportunities for growth, so with help from his wife, Mary, and stepson, Stacey, he decided to build a town. He chose the name Centerville because it would be the "central point" between Kalama and Tacoma. Mary Jane named several streets, including Pearl, Diamond, Gold, and Locust. They planned the center of the town around the establishments of Wingard, Crosby, and Young, which were near present-day Tower Avenue and Main Street. By 1873, they started construction.

After years of planning, they brought their plat, which consisted of just four blocks and a town name, to the courthouse in Saundersville, present-day Chehalis. They filed the plat for Centerville on January 8, 1875. Washington pledged to sell only to people who wanted to settle in Centerville, not to someone who would leave after only a few years. To ensure the quality of the lots, Washington hired surveyors. He sold the first hundred or so lots for five dollars each if the owner erected a building worth at least one hundred dollars. He later sold lots for ten dollars each. Within a year, the population totaled fifty.

After officially founding the city of Centerville, the Washingtons continued to seek new opportunities to grow their town. In the summer of 1875, Washington donated land for a Baptist church and assisted with its construction. He also donated a few acres of his farmland for a cemetery, where he buried his parents and where he rests today.

By 1878, the population of Centerville had reached about seventy. The railroad made transporting lumber and other goods and equipment easier. In 1880, Centerville possessed the only train depot between Kalama and Tacoma, theoretically making it a prime spot for travelers to stop. On November 8, 1881, George Washington platted the first addition to the town, which included more roads and a public square, now known as George Washington Park.

In 1883, the name Centerville changed to Centralia largely to avoid confusion with a town of the same name in Eastern Washington. David Fouts, a newcomer who originated from Centralia, Illinois, suggested the new name. A.W. Height built the first mill in the city. Sawmills, shingle mills, and lumbermills became significant sources of jobs and income. By 1884, the population reached two hundred, and the next year saw the rise of the first weekly newspaper, *The Centralia News*. In 1886, Washington leased lots to James Agnew who used the land for a store and restaurant.

The Washington Territorial Legislature created the city of Centralia at a legislative assembly on January 27, 1886, when the town boasted a population of 325 people. The government consisted of a five-member board of trustees with a board president. They were sworn into office on February 12, 1886. Two years later, the Ballard and Bond mill opened; this mill became the largest mill ever operated in Centralia after its purchase by F.B. Hubbard, who renamed it Eastern Railway and Lumber Co in 1903.

The year 1889 proved historic in the Pacific Northwest as Washington became the forty-second state in the United States of America on November 11, 1889. Closer to home, George and Mary Washington leased land for a hospital outside the city limits. The population had reached nine hundred. *The Centralia Chronicle* newspaper started operating, and A.J. Miller opened the city's first financial institution, the Bank of California. George built Washington Hotel on Tower Avenue—the brick hotel featured full electricity and an elevator. Centralia's voters unanimously decided to surrender the existing town charter and reincorporate under a new one. On February 13, 1889, voters elected a new board chairman, and officers were appointed as town clerk, treasurer, marshal, assessor, street commissioner, and town attorney. The board set up committees to oversee streets, auditing and finance, sanitary regulation and health, and fire and water.

But they weren't happy with the setup, so in January 1890, voters switched to a mayor-council form of government with a mayor elected citywide and six councilors elected from wards or neighborhoods within the city. They selected George T. Swasey as the first mayor and also voted to reincorporate as a third-class city. The council elected a city clerk, marshal, night watchman, and city attorney.

The city experienced a huge expansion in the following few years. Since its start as Centerville in 1875, the town had grown to cover nearly three square miles. With abundant timber nearby, the city capitalized on logging and milling lumber. Several mills opened. Furniture, hardware, pump, brick, and soda companies cropped up in the city and surrounding area. Coal mining at nearby Tono and Mendota became another source of employment. Hay, barley, oats, and hops were among the agricultural commodities.

In 1891, a railway company built a line that ran through the main stretch of town to the Skookumchuck River. The first telephones arrived in the city. George Dysart was replaced by G.B. Richmond as the city's judge. October brought the region's first recorded fair. The population hit 5,000.

Despite its phenomenal growth, Centralia faced a new challenge in 1893. The economy crashed. Across the country, thousands lost their jobs, and banks and railroads closed. In Centralia, the population plummeted. Mills, factories, and railroads slowed or shut down altogether. Trains burned wood instead of coal or electricity, so people earned money logging to fuel the trains with wood.

As businesses shut their doors, people left the city in droves. The once-booming population of 5,000 just two years prior rapidly dwindled to 1,200.

To support his "town people," as he called them, George Washington purchased large amounts of basic food items, ordered shoes, and provided work. He never pressed for rent payments or collections on debts owed to him and did not collect interest when the payments were finally made. He purchased property only if the owners wanted to sell. He made sure no one went hungry, unclothed, or without work.

Throughout the crash, the city still grew. On January 15, 1895, the city bought the Centralia Electric Light and Power Company plant. A month later, the city voted to allow public electricity in Centralia. In December 1896, the volunteer fire department officially incorporated.

George Washington's dedication to his city and his people allowed Centralia to recover after the economic crash ended in 1898. The town and its people were ready to turn the page into the next century.

LEWIS COUNTY HISTORICAL MUSEUM PC162

The caption says, "Logging in the '60s" at Centralia, Washington—that's 1860s, not 1960s.

LEWIS COUNTY HISTORICAL MUSEUM P179

Although they lived on the frontier, Centerville residents wanted their children to learn. The photo above shows the community's first school, a one-room building that operated only three months of the year. Teachers Mrs. Wingard, Mrs. Canby, and W.A. Peters can be seen standing in back. Notable student surnames include Agnew, Crosby, Davis, Mills, Saunders, Wingard, and Young. Below is South School (later Lincoln Elementary) built in 1889 on land donated by George Washington.

LEWIS COUNTY HISTORICAL MUSEUM P2362

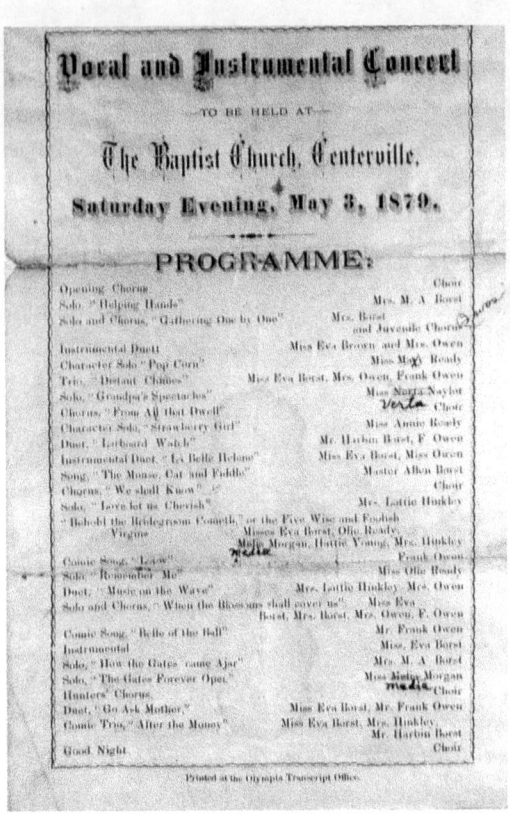

LEWIS COUNTY HISTORICAL MUSEUM P12828

At left is the May 3, 1879, program for the Vocal and Instrumental Concert at the Centerville Baptist Church. Below is an undated postcard showing the First Baptist Church on Pine and Pearl constructed in the 1890s. Fire destroyed the building in the late 1920s, and a church of brick was constructed in its place but was no longer used as a church by 1971.

LEWIS COUNTY HISTORICAL MUSEUM PC1721

LEWIS COUNTY HISTORICAL MUSEUM P4727

LEWIS COUNTY HISTORICAL MUSEUM P8527

LEWIS COUNTY HISTORICAL MUSEUM P4668

The photo above from the 1880s shows Centerville, also known as Centralia, with dirt roads and buildings along the main street, including the Tin Shop, the Racket Store, and the first State Bank of Centralia, which later became known as the Matz building and Lewis County State Bank. Damaged in the 1949 earthquake, the building was destroyed in a 2012 fire. At left are photos showing the town as Centerville. The community erected an arch in honr of a visit by Henry Villard, presidnet of Northern Pacific Railroad, in 1883. Centralia residents believed he would stop at the train depot because it was the only one between the Puget Sound and Portland. However, his train just chugged on by.

LEWIS COUNTY HISTORICAL MUSEUM P11500

On Independence Day, July 4, 1885, Centralia founder George Washington dressed in a Knights Templar uniform. He can be seen on a platform in the back right of the photo. At right, Dr. Edward Truesdell, a dentist involved in the Southwest Washington Fair and harness racing, is seen with a patient. He opened his practice in Centralia around 1890 above the Churchill Glove Factory on Maple Street, then moved to the first Proffitt's Department Store on Tower and Magnolia. The photo below is labeled, "The Old Way of Logging, Centralia, Wash."

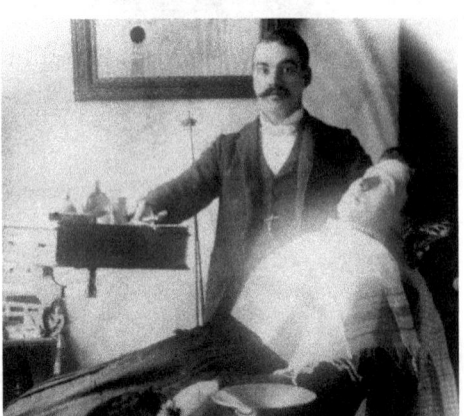

LEWIS COUNTY HISTORICAL MUSEUM P8183

LEWIS COUNTY HISTORICAL MUSEUM PC1884

LEWIS COUNTY HISTORICAL MUSEUM P77

As the city grew, so did the places for people to worship. Above is an Easter Sunday 1890 photo of St. John's Episcopal Church on First Street. Below is an 1891 photo of the Methodist Church on Gold Street.

LEWIS COUNTY HISTORICAL MUSEUM P9917

LEWIS COUNTY HISTORICAL MUSEUM P8525

Above, Centralia Baptist Grace Seminary School, later the Centralia Hospital, in the late 1800s with students on the front porch before remodeling removed the lattice work. Below is a photo of Centralia's first train depot, taken in 1892.

LEWIS COUNTY HISTORICAL MUSEUM P4662

LEWIS COUNTY HISTORICAL MUSEUM P11586

LEWIS COUNTY HISTORICAL MUSEUM P18488

Above, an undated photo shows a driver hauling hay on Tower Avene. At left is The Depot Hotel between First and Second. From left are Justice Conrad, his second wife, Alvira Tovey Conrad, Wally Conrad, and Flossie Conrad. Below, cars are parked outside The Depot Hotel near the train station.

LEWIS COUNTY HISTORICAL MUSEUM P15683

Young Abbott Townsend, left, stands next to another man in the 1890s. Townsend was born on June 17, 1868, in California. After arriving in Centralia on November 14, 1879, he and his parents resided at the Pioneer Hotel for a decade before moving into their house on Thanksgiving Day in 1889. That year, he and his family ate spareribs and mashed potatoes for dinner. At eighty-six, Townsend recalled that no families had turkey in those days. Below is a photo circa 1900 of seventeen men on a steam engine at a logging operation site.

PHOTO COURTESY OF ISAAC HARJO

LEWIS COUNTY HISTORICAL MUSEUM P12279

This 1902 photo shows Abbott Townsend, then age thirty-four, sprawled in the undercut of a large tree in Salzer Valley. Two other loggers stand on either side of the tree. Townsend worked as a logger, farmer, railroad crewman, and saw filer in his adulthood. Below, a photo taken in 1893 north of Centralia depicts loggers with their tools. Logging was a huge industry in the area and became especially vital during the depression that began the year this photo was taken.

PHOTO COURTESY OF ISAAC HARJO

LEWIS COUNTY HISTORICAL MUSEUM P10874

LEWIS COUNTY HISTORICAL MUSEUM P6054

These photos from Paul Davies show the bank building on the corner of Tower and Main Streets circa 1890 when it was the Lewis County Bank. Doctors Bietl and Heine, physicians and surgeons, had offices upstairs. Below is an interior view of a bank showing the tellers windows. Note the spitoon on the floor.

LEWIS COUNTY HISTORICAL MUSEUM P6052.

LEWIS COUNTY HISTORICAL MUSEUM P20756

CITY HALL, CENTRALIA, WASH.

LEWIS COUNTY HISTORICAL MUSEUM P8699

Above, this 1898 photo shows Spanish-American War veterans in formation near the corner of West Main Street and Tower Avenue. Signs for a restaurant and hardware store are visible. At left is a rare photo of the Centralia City Hall and Fire Department before 1906. Below, a drawing shows C. Crosby General Merchandise Store in Centralia at the corner of Locust and Tower in 1880. It also shows Johnson Drug Store and E.R. Butterworth Furniture and Undertaking.

LEWIS COUNTY HISTORICAL MUSEUM P1457

LEWIS COUNTY HISTORICAL MUSEUM P2243

Before the construction of bridges over the Chehalis River, ferries transported people and cargo across the river, such as at Galvin, likely pictured above, and Lincoln Creek northwest of Centralia, below, in about 1896. The ferry is carrying a four-wheeled flatbed wagon loaded with bundles of cedar shakes and drawn by two horses. Cables across the river and a dock on each side of the river were used to pull the ferry.

LEWIS COUNTY HISTORICAL MUSEUM P2683

LEWIS COUNTY HISTORICAL MUSEUM P11662

Above is the 700 block of Washington Avenue in Centralia with an unpaved road and a horse-drawn buggy in the background with a few unidentified people on the sidewalk. Below is a photo of the Whealdon house, built around 1900, located near the Galvin Bridge.

LEWIS COUNTY HISTORICAL MUSEUM P12879

LEWIS COUNTY HISTORICAL MUSEUM P12277

Loggers sit near a steam engine at a logging site near Centralia in the late 1800s or early 1900s. Below is a train locomotive with its crew about the same time period. The depot was a great source of employment to local men.

LEWIS COUNTY HISTORICAL MUSEUM P8265

LEWIS COUNTY HISTORICAL MUSEUM P11575

A horse-drawn fire wagon with two unidentified men in uniforms leave the fire station, above. Near the rear of the wagon is another unidentified man in uniform. Below is the interior of a butcher shop in Centralia.

LEWIS COUNTY HISTORICAL MUSEUM P1012

LEWIS COUNTY HISTORICAL MUSEUM P1810   LEWIS COUNTY HISTORICAL MUSEUM P1809

Isabella (Brown) Phelps, left, and her husband, Joseph Phelps, were early settlers on Lincoln Creek northwest of Centralia. Through the decades, many people in the Lincoln Creek area earned a living by farming, logging, or working in sawmills. Below is an undated photo of George Foglesong and his son Bert harvesting hay at Lincoln Creek.

LEWIS COUNTY HISTORICAL MUSEUM P10791

LEWIS COUNTY HISTORICAL MUSEUM P10259

Workers above are building the Lincoln Creek Bridge in February 1899. Below, men with logging tools work in the Hanaford Valley.

LEWIS COUNTY HISTORICAL MUSEUM P10799

LEWIS COUNTY HISTORICAL MUSEUM P4549

Above is the old Centralia High School, which served students until a new building was constructed in the early 1900s. Below, several men surround a large tree, some holding axes. The photo inscription says, "9 Foot Cedar, Western Wash."

LEWIS COUNTY HISTORICAL MUSEUM P21581

LEWIS COUNTY HISTORICAL MUSEUM P10875

Three men work on felling a tree with a crosscut saw near Centralia.

LEWIS COUNTY HISTORICAL MUSEUM P55

Grace Seminary, shortly after its construction, and its plank walkway. Construction began on the Baptist seminary in 1885 on property owned by a local church, which turned it over to the Northwest Convention of Baptists. Construction of the hilltop school cost more than $15,000 (equivalent to more than $532,000 today). The three-story building had four chambers, a full basement, dining room, kitchen, pantry, wood room, laundry, and two bathrooms. It started as a church school that could serve thirty-six students and later became a preparatory school, but economic issues plagued it. The prep school closed but the building reopened in 1900 as another school before serving as a general hospital. Then it was abandoned for years until wreckers in 1938 demolished it to build a new National Guard Armory.

Five

A Booming New Century

Despite the generosity of founder George Washington in rescuing the city from total annihilation during the economic downturn of 1893, Centralia lost residents at the height of the panic but rebounded a bit by the end of the century. The population dropped from 2,026 in 1890 to 1,600 in 1900, according to census records.

But the new millennium dawned with the promise of renewed hope in the Hub City halfway between the Columbia River and Puget Sound, a hub where four railroad lines and two rivers met, a town that survived the depression through the largesse of its founder. And the first decade of the twentieth century boosted the city's population to 7,311 by 1910.

Although the city government changed frequently during the city's early years, it had settled into a mayor-council form of government, which sufficed for two decades. But in the fall of 1911, voters switched to a commission form of government with a mayor—the first being H.W. Thompson with John Galvin not long after him—and two commissioners, one overseeing finances and the other public works.

At the dawn of the twentieth century, the council's biggest issue was preventing hogs and cattle from wandering city streets.

The battle over the sale of alcohol proved one of the biggest issues facing the city in the early part of the twentieth century. The temperance movement flourished with petitioners seeking a "dry" city rather than a "wet" one filled

75

with thirty-five saloons on Tower Avenue alone. The Legislature adopted a Sunday closing law. The issue became moot with the passage of the Eighteenth Amendment to the U.S. Constitution on January 16, 1919, which instituted Prohibition, a ban on the sale of alcoholic beverages that lasted until 1933, when the amendment was repealed.

Loggers, millworkers, and miners found jobs plentiful in the woods and coal mines around Centralia. Men worked farms, raised cattle, and grew fruit. By 1906, six coal mines shipped the black ore from Centralia, including those in Tono and soon Mendota, thriving communities with hotels, company stores, and post offices. Centralia had seven sawmills in 1910, including the largest one, Eastern Railway and Lumber Company, which was organized in 1903. Sam Agnew worked for the company, owned stock in it, and eventually oversaw operations as general manager. Two years after fire destroyed the Eastern Mill in 1939, Sam and Jay Agnew formed S.A. Agnew Lumber Company, leasing Western Mill property from the Eastern Railway and Lumber Company, and began operations in 1941. At its peak, Agnew employed about four hundred people, but it closed in 1959.

Centralia schools taught 950 students in 1902, a number that grew to 1,600 students eight years later, and enrollment totaled 2,450 by 1916, when forty-six seniors graduated from Centralia High School. The district built Washington School in 1910 and taught high school students there until completion of the new high school in 1912.

Centralia's infrastructure continued to improve. The Centralia Electric Light Company provided light, heat, and power and expanded distribution throughout the city by erecting power poles and stringing lines.

The city built a new water reservoir on Seminary Hill and later a municipal gravity system using water from the North Fork of the Newaukum River. In the early 1900s, the city installed water mains and fire hydrants in the city.

In 1906, the city replaced old wooden sidewalks in the northwest quarter with concrete. The poor condition of Tower Avenue demanded attention with mud up to five inches deep, so city officials spread gravel on it in 1902, first hiring workers to remove the mud and install fir planks. People drove around stumps in some streets. By 1908, the city had paved Tower and part of Main Street with bricks. City officials started building a sewage system in 1907, and the health officer suggested regular garbage collection to curtail the spread of disease. Tuberculosis accounted for one in every five deaths.

The old telephone system installed in 1891 needed work, and Sunset Telephone Company linemen strung new cable in the city. Then, in 1908,

Pacific Telephone Company constructed a new system to serve a thousand homes and businesses. In 1910, the Washington-Oregon Corp., which operated a light and power company on Coal Creek, opened an electric railway to serve the Twin Cities.

The city's volunteer fire department, which first organized on May 15, 1890, disbanded in July 1908, when the city hired paid firefighters. That's the same year the City Council created an automobile ordinance.

While initially the city hired a couple of marshals to maintain law and order, in January 1904, the city created the Centralia Police Department, which had ten members who shared their headquarters with firefighters in a two-story wooden building at Tower and Magnolia. By 1910, the city constructed a concrete and brick jail on West Maple Street, which was torn down in 1921 during construction of a new modern brick City Hall, which also housed police officers and firefighters until construction of a new fire station on North Pearl in 1955. The city installed parking meters downtown in 1949 but removed them before the 1980s.

Early in the century, a new opera house was constructed in Centralia, and a new train schedule enabled people to travel to Olympia and back the same day. The Centralia Driving Association scheduled horse races in May 1906. More than five hundred people showed up for opening day of the races at the driving park. But someone poisoned Red Bird, a favorite horse.

Farmers gathered at city hall to discuss forming a Grange in town. And Eastern Railway and Lumber Company petitioned the postal service for a post office designation at the Wilson coal mines nine miles outside of town.

Civil War veteran David Fouts, who raised livestock on Yelm Prairie, was considered one of Centralia's early leaders. He bought property from George Washington, paying forty-five dollars for a block in the area where Edison theater later stood, and sold it for ten times as much. The next buyer sold the property for five thousand dollars. Fouts also opened a butcher shop in town and opened the first dray business to move freight by wagons and carts.

In 1916, tickets to the Grand Theater cost between fifty cents and $1.50. Ray Loomis, a night yard foreman at the railroad, died in Tacoma after both legs were severed when an engine ran over him. A religious revival packed the Centralia tabernacle.

A weeklong Hub City Festival took place in 1912, celebrating completion of the Carnegie Library, the new train depot, and movement of the post office from a small building at Main and Tower into the newly completed Dumon Building at Pearl and Main.

Residents turned out to cheer on Claude Berlin, the city's first flier, who graduated from Curtiss Flying School. He staged an exhibition in 1912 and planned to christen new buildings by dropping bottles of champagne from his plane onto the new library, train depot, and Dumon building, although educators said they didn't want a champagne bottle dropped on the new high school. He missed the library and Dumon building, and the bottle that hit the depot broke roof tiles, but he landed his aircraft safely. By 1928, Centralia even boasted of its own airport with a hangar at Borst Park, but after the Chehalis-Centralia airport opened, flight activity near Borst Park slowed, and by the mid-1930s, the municipal air field closed.

A bank failure in 1914 caused a hiccup in the economy attributed to a slump in the timber market, and tensions grew between union workers and citizens who favored a free capitalist society. The friction hit home in Centralia during a Red Cross parade in 1918 when a raid on the headquarters of the Industrial Workers of the World left the building ransacked, furniture burned, and union activists beaten and dumped outside the city.

As World War I (WWI) in Europe grew more intense, Lewis County boys from Company M prepared to sail overseas. They had fought against revolutionary Pancho Villa in Mexico in 1916 and quelled violence involving union activists from the Industrial Workers of the World on the Everett docks in November of that year. The United States entered World War I—the so-called "war to end all wars"—on April 6, 1917, and local troops fought the Germans with the American and British forces.

Many never returned home.

LEWIS COUNTY HISTORICAL MUSEUM P17451

The Centralia Community Hall on North Tower, which included the police and fire departments, is seen in the early 1900s. Below is a log farmhouse that originally belonged to Joseph Remley, a man who settled on Waunch Prairie in 1860. Lucy Anne Remley Whealdon married William Whealdon. The home was later owned by the Kaestner family. From left, daughter Beva Whealdon Stahl, Anna Remley Whealdon, son Joe Whealdon, and William Whealdon.

LEWIS COUNTY HISTORICAL MUSEUM P8632

LEWIS COUNTY HISTORICAL MUSEUM P18721

Above is the Centralia Hotel on Main Street with a hotel carriage and team to transport guests. One passenger is inside with the driver ready to go. A postman and others stand nearby, circa 1900. Below, a parade in Centralia to celebrate the end of the Spanish-American War on December 10, 1898.

LEWIS COUNTY HISTORICAL MUSEUM P11598

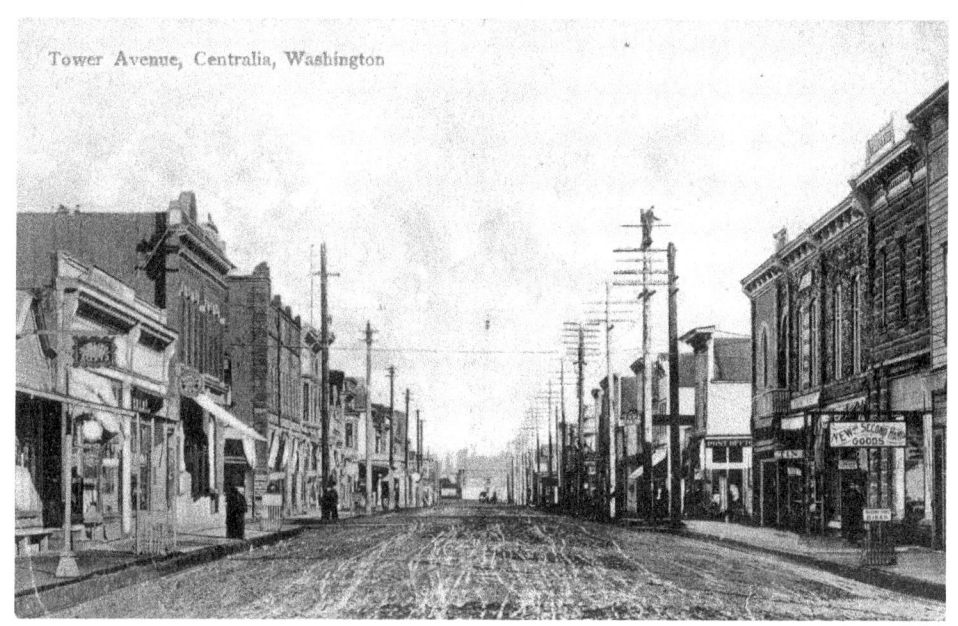

LEWIS COUNTY HISTORICAL MUSEUM PC2419

Above is a black-and-white print of Tower Avenue in Centralia near Main Street looking north at the dawn of the twentieth century. The Post Office sign can be seen along with a shingle for a second-hand store. Below, the city park today known as George Washington Park can be seen before the construction of the Carnegie Library in 1912. The photo shows a walkway and gazebo. The photo was taken looking west toward the Centralia Hotel.

LEWIS COUNTY HISTORICAL MUSEUM P4333

LEWIS COUNTY HISTORICAL MUSEUM P20500

Several men and a team of horses haul logs near Centralia in 1900. Archie L.A. Davis, the man on the horse, was one of the first members of the Lewis County Agricultural Association in 1882. Below, in the early 1900s, men with the Lincoln Creek Lumber Company (and a dog) sit on a steam donkey, a machine designed to drag logs from the woods to a landing.

LEWIS COUNTY HISTORICAL MUSEUM P10968

LEWIS COUNTY HISTORICAL MUSEUM P6296

Above is a photo of the Chehalis River bridge at Galvin during its construction. A ferry operated upstream of the bridge during its construction. After it opened, people on horseback were fined five dollars if they rode faster than they could walk because fast galloping could damage the suspension bridge. The bridge has since been updated to sturdier concrete. The Eastern Railway and Lumber was among the region's largest employers at the dawn of the twentieth century. Below, workers for the Eastern Railway and Lumber Company lay tracks and operate steam engine.

LEWIS COUNTY HISTORICAL MUSEUM P12274

LEWIS COUNTY HISTORICAL MUSEUM P8116

The top photo shows a wrecked logging train thought to be near Centralia around the 1900s. At left, Childers and Ogle Logging harvests logs near Lincoln Creek in the early 1900s.

LEWIS COUNTY HISTORICAL MUSEUM P10879

LEWIS COUNTY HISTORICAL MUSEUM P1441

The 1904 photo above shows a logging camp set up by C. W. Geiger at Galvin, Washington. At left, Joe and Abe Garrison wield axes in 1907 while standing on springboards as Archie Davis leans on tree.

LEWIS COUNTY HISTORICAL MUSEUM P20499

PHOTOS COURTESY OF GRACE GRANT

During the early 1900s, Centralia saw immense growth in the population, which rose from 1,600 at the dawn of the century to 7,311 a decade later. Among the newcomers were George and Susanna Cambridge, left, who set out from Nampa, Idaho, in 1905 with their family and all their belongings in the photo above.

PHOTO COURTESY OF GRACE GRANT

The photo above shows the Cambridge family's house on H Street in Centralia. Below is a 1907 photo of Palace Market with Ira and Jim Luman behind the counter. Christmas decorations hang from the ceiling and meat hangs from hooks on the wall.

LEWIS COUNTY HISTORICAL MUSEUM P11608

LEWIS COUNTY HISTORICAL MUSEUM PC2827

Jobs drew newcomers to Centralia with the promise of work in the woods, the mines, the mills, or businesses like Churchill Glove Factory, seen in the photo above in the early 1900s. Below, a family stands in front of a large log house at the Dr. Francis camp at Galvin. From left, Edith, Clea, Lee, and Minnie Scranton. Edith and Minnie were sisters, and Minnie was the mother of Clea and Lee.

LEWIS COUNTY HISTORICAL MUSEUM P4640

LEWIS COUNTY HISTORICAL MUSEUM P21109

Above is the Chehalis River Bridge near Galvin. Below, Dr. David Livingstone can be seen in the operating room at Centralia Hospital on Seminary Hill, sometime between 1907 and 1913. He is holding a scalpel and looking down at the patient.

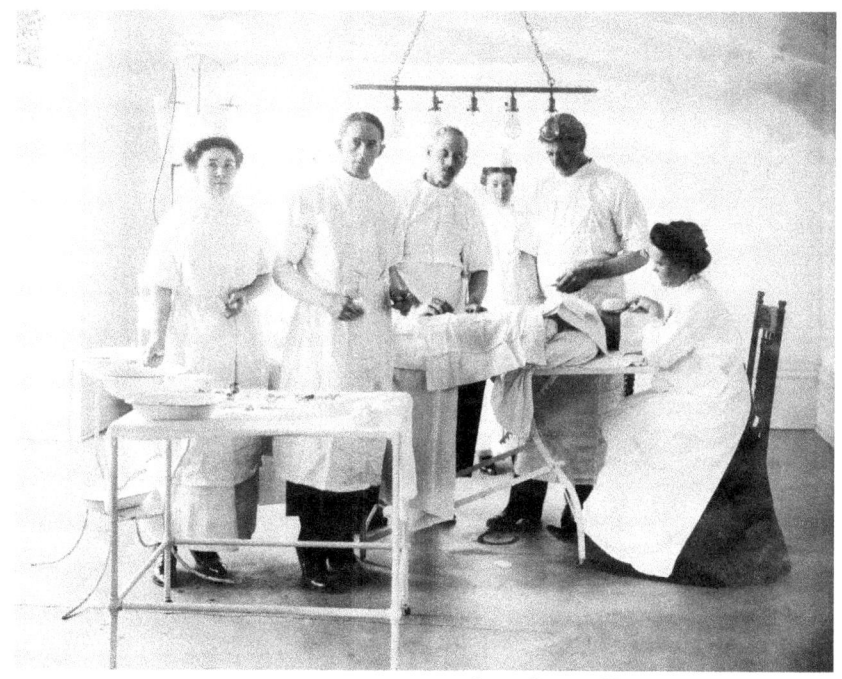

LEWIS COUNTY HISTORICAL MUSEUM P1020

LEWIS COUNTY HISTORICAL MUSEUM P16056

Members of the Centralia Volunteer Fire Department do a demonstration on North Tower in 1907 as the volunteers practice with the hose cart. Constable Henry Shields stands on the sidewalk. Below is a 1911 photo of a Seagrove firetruck and uniformed firefighters.

LEWIS COUNTY HISTORICAL MUSEUM P11648

LEWIS COUNTY HISTORICAL MUSEUM P20517

Schuyler Colfax Davis, fourth from left wearing a derby hat, stands with the 1908 Centralia City Council, firefighters, and police officers. The third man from the left in front is Centralia Mayor John Guerrier. Below, in 1910, workers install tracks for a trolley in downtown Centralia. The Olympic Club and the Palace Market are visible on right side of photo.

LEWIS COUNTY HISTORICAL MUSEUM P11551

LEWIS COUNTY HISTORICAL MUSEUM P11570

These photos show two different views of the trolley running on North Tower Avenue in Centralia. The photo above, looking north, shows the Post Office on the corner and two people riding bicycles up the street with the trolley in the background. Pedestrians at right are on a sidewalk with the Olympic Club in background. The photo below shows Tower Avenue, looking south at the street car, City Hall, and the fire station along the dirt road.

LEWIS COUNTY HISTORICAL MUSEUM PC2428

LEWIS COUNTY HISTORICAL MUSEUM P948

Four men ride in an open horse-drawn buggy in Washington Park about 1908. From left, they are James McCash, Charles Sticklin, Fred Thomas, and Dr. Bozarth, a Centralia veterinarian. Below is a bird's-eye view of Centralia's north end about 1910.

LEWIS COUNTY HISTORICAL MUSEUM P8343

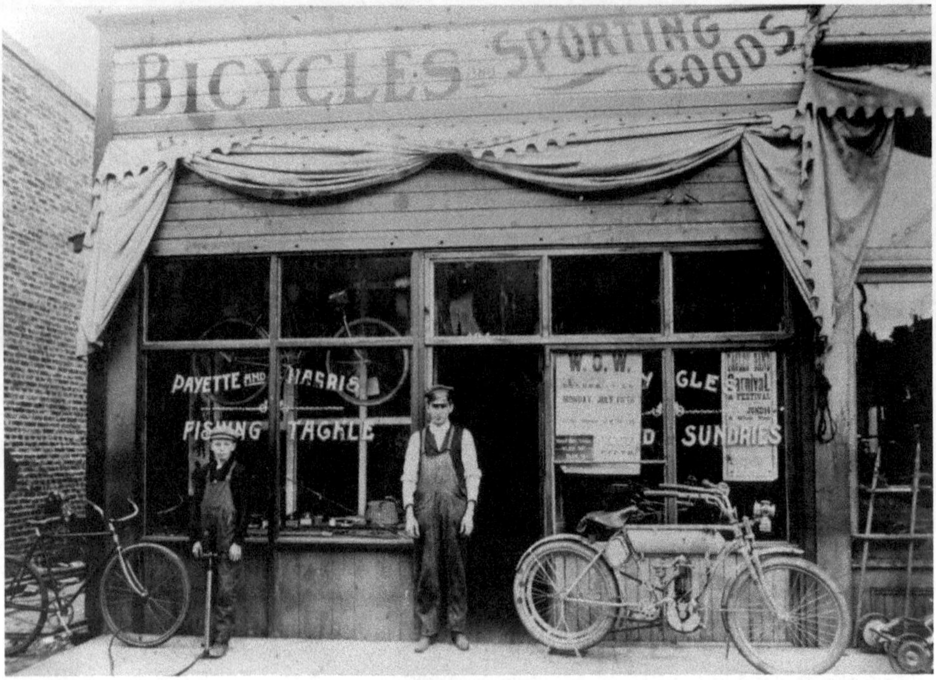

Lewis County Historical Museum P11621

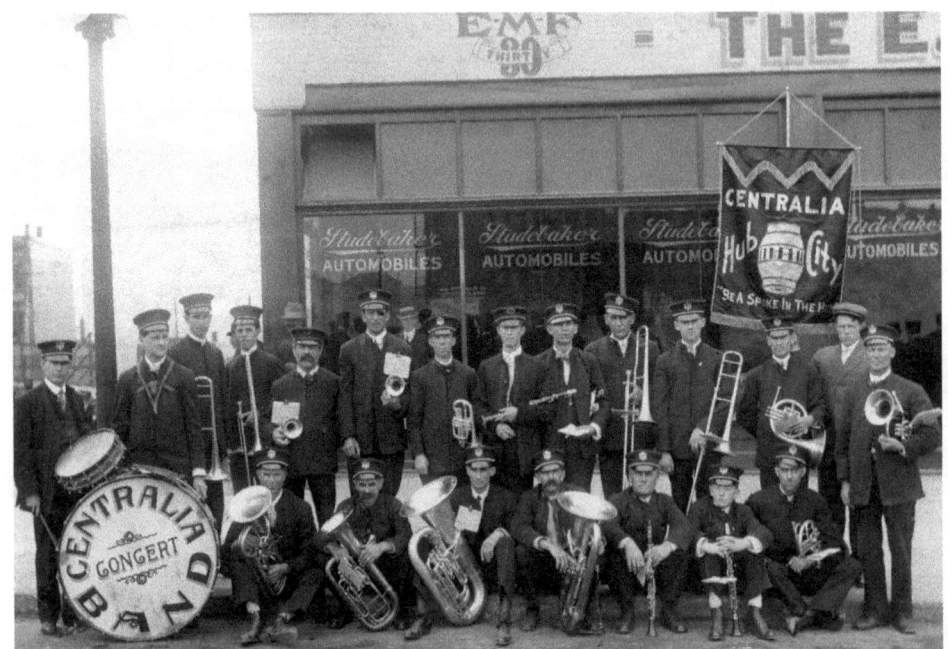

Above is an undated photo of the Payette and Harris Bicycle and Sporting Goods Shop. Below, the Centralia Concert Band performs in front of Studebaker Automobiles in 1911.

Lewis County Historical Museum P2980

LEWIS COUNTY HISTORICAL MUSEUM P6056

The interior of Centralia's National Bank above shows unidentified bank employees with several tellers cages, circa 1890–1910. Below is a 1908 photo of Bars Clothing.

LEWIS COUNTY HISTORICAL MUSEUM P1011

The photo above from the early 1910s shows the interior of a hardware store in Centralia with unidentified employees and customers. The postcard below dated February 9, 1913, shows the interior of the Centralia Seed Store in the 100 block of Tower Avenue. The man standing near the floor scale beneath the huge Pyramid Flour sign is apparently owner or operator of store.

LEWIS COUNTY HISTORICAL MUSEUM P8363

The old high school became Edison School as seen in this photo from the early 1900s. Below, the new Washington School was built in 1906 near Gold and Plum Streets. It was replaced in 1950.

LEWIS COUNTY HISTORICAL MUSEUM P4334

LEWIS COUNTY HISTORICAL MUSEUM P20733

In 1903, the city dedicated its second Methodist Church at Pine and Pearl Streets. The program for laying the cornerstone of the Methodist Episcopal Church featured the Reverend J.W. Miller as noted in the program below, which shows the event took place from May 29 to May 31, 1903.

Program

For the Cornerstone Laying of the Methodist Episcopal Church, of Centralia, Wash., May 29-31, '03.

All former and neighboring pastors invited to be present.

All contributors desired to be present with their families.

All members of the church expected to be present with their families.

J. W. MILLER, PASTOR.

LEWIS COUNTY HISTORICAL MUSEUM P11539

LEWIS COUNTY HISTORICAL MUSEUM P19242

Above is a 1910 photo of St. Mary's Roman Catholic Church on Washington Avenue. At left, from the early 1900s is a photo of the Church of the Brethren on Gold Street, which George Washington built as a Baptist Church but Ezra Whisler purchased in 1902.

LEWIS COUNTY HISTORICAL MUSEUM P1645

LEWIS COUNTY HISTORICAL MUSEUM P3182

The photo from around 1912 shows the First Presbyterian Church on the corner of Rock and Pine Streets. The photo also shows dirt roads muddy with rain and the transition from plank board sidewalks to concrete. The church was torn down at a later time.

LEWIS COUNTY HISTORICAL MUSEUM PC1904

The early 1900s brought new construction throughout Centralia. Above is the new Centralia High School, which was built in 1912. Below is the new Carnegie Library in Washington Park with a gazebo on the left. It was constructed in 1911, using a grant from Scottish-American businessman Andrew Carnegie, who funded 2,509 libraries built between 1883 and 1929. Music was played in the gazebo during holiday festivities, especially on July 4th.

LEWIS COUNTY HISTORICAL MUSEUM P4798

101

The new Centralia Union Depot, above and right, opened in 1912 and matched the one built in Chehalis, so they became known as the "Twin Depots." The photo at lower right shows the Centralia Round House and Railroad Yard with tracks and cars. When the Round House was torn down later, bricks were sold, and some were incorporated into the face of a home at 319 Willow Lane on Plummer Lake.

LEWIS COUNTY HISTORICAL MUSEUM P17121

LEWIS COUNTY HISTORICAL MUSEUM P4664

LEWIS COUNTY HISTORICAL MUSEUM P2638

A train stops by the Centralia Union Depot, which opened on June 1, 1912. At this point, trains used diesel instead of steam. Below is an undated photo of men in a bowling alley in Centralia.

LEWIS COUNTY HISTORICAL MUSEUM P11622

LEWIS COUNTY HISTORICAL MUSEUM P11649

Above, Claude Berlin, the city's first aviator, and Gennette Salkick Miller sit on his airship "Centralia" in 1912 at the Southwest Washington Fairgrounds. He christened new buildings in Centralia by dropping champagne bottles from the air but missed.

LEWIS COUNTY HISTORICAL MUSEUM P1643

LEWIS COUNTY HISTORICAL MUSEUM P6433

Genette Salick Miller christened Claude Berlin's airship "Centralia" at the Southwest Washington Fairgrounds on May 31, 1912. He is seen below sitting on the "Centralia" at the Southwest Washington Fairgrounds in August 1912. Residents turned out to cheer on Berlin, who graduated from Curtiss Flying School, when he planned to christen new buildings by dropping bottles of champagne from his plane. He missed the library and Dumon building, and the bottle that hit the depot broke roof tiles.

LEWIS COUNTY HISTORICAL MUSEUM P1642

LEWIS COUNTY HISTORICAL MUSEUM P20540

The entrance to the new Centralia High School, above, and a glimpse inside at the entry landing, looking up the stairs on either side.

LEWIS COUNTY HISTORICAL MUSEUM P4649

LEWIS COUNTY HISTORICAL MUSEUM P4650

Centralia High School interior in 1914 with a view looking down the stairs to the entrance. Below is a view of the new school's Domestic Science Kitchen. Girls worked in pairs with two gas plates, an individual oven and cupboards which contained their cooking utensils and supplies.

LEWIS COUNTY HISTORICAL MUSEUM P4651

LEWIS COUNTY HISTORICAL MUSEUM P4652

Inside the high school in 1914. The top photo shows the Domestic Science Sewing Room. At left is the drawing and art room, and below is the woodshop.

LEWIS COUNTY HISTORICAL MUSEUM P4653

LEWIS COUNTY HISTORICAL MUSEUM P4654

LEWIS COUNTY HISTORICAL MUSEUM P11647

The photo above was taken in front of the City Hall and Fire Department in Centralia on July 4th, 1912. The building is decorated with American flag banners. The 1910 photo below shows the first car in Centralia, owned by Claude Carter, the man behind the wheel. The Baptist Church can be seen in the background.

LEWIS COUNTY HISTORICAL MUSEUM PC1177

LEWIS COUNTY HISTORICAL MUSEUM P10559

The 1915 photo above shows workers at the Farmers' Cooperative Creamery Company making butter. Below, Daniel Webster Leonard is at his secondhand and dry goods store on North Tower.

LEWIS COUNTY HISTORICAL MUSEUM P18597

LEWIS COUNTY HISTORICAL MUSEUM P10556

W. F. Kelling, manager of Farmers' Cooperative Creamery Company, is with Ray T. Evans in 1915 at the office at North Pearl Street and West Fifth in Centralia. The company produced butter and dealt in hay, grain, flour, and feed. Below is an undated photo of Eubanks Leather Shop.

LEWIS COUNTY HISTORICAL MUSEUM P11610

PHOTOS COURTESY OF GRACE GRANT

During a spring 1916 trip, the Cambridge family ran across a motorist whose car was stuck in the early spring mud. They tried to pull him out and got their rig stuck temporarilty before managing to free both from the muck. On the back of the photo postcard, a writer explains what happened, writing, "We had some good times. The old folks enjoy them as much as we do." The photo below of Ivy Camp No. 1982 members from Centralia. On April 13, 1916, The Daily Hub *explained how Mrs. W. S. Grass was surprised after a walk with a friend to find Aid Society of Ivy Camp, R.N.A. members inside, ready to celebrate her birthday. In 1914, the Ivy Camp members founded the Aid Society in Mrs. Grass's home. Mrs. Cambridge, who was present at this gathering, helped prepare a lunch.*

LEWIS COUNTY HISTORICAL MUSEUM P19911

The photo above taken in September 1908 near Centralia shows several men sitting on a log and one with a horse. Below, loggers are seen near a steam engine and fallen timber in the 1910s. The photo inscription says, "Logging scene, Centralia, Wash."

LEWIS COUNTY HISTORICAL MUSEUM PC1886

LEWIS COUNTY HISTORICAL MUSEUM P12269

The 1910 photo shows an Eastern Railway and Lumber Company logging crew at Mendota. Below is the Eastern Railway and Lumber Company headquarters covered in snow in Centralia. This building was constructed in the early 1910s.

LEWIS COUNTY HISTORICAL MUSEUM P17307

Dozens of men stand in front of a mill with logs floating in the water. The photo was likely taken near Centralia in 1909.

LEWIS COUNTY HISTORICAL MUSEUM P8122

LEWIS COUNTY HISTORICAL MUSEUM P11654

The photo above is of the Eastern Mill. The inscription says, "No. 29 Scene at Saw Mill, Centralia, Wash." The photo below of the Eastern Mill shows its proximity to the railroad yards.

LEWIS COUNTY HISTORICAL MUSEUM P842

LEWIS COUNTY HISTORICAL MUSEUM P2566

An excellent photo entitled "A Mountain Road" by O.A. Nelson (1913) shows Michigan Hill Road in the Lincoln Creek area, west of Centralia, as it appeared in earlier times when travel was mainly by horse and buggy. It won first place in the black-and-white division of the 1913 Southwest Washington Fair.

LEWIS COUNTY HISTORICAL MUSEUM P20502

Loggers on Davis Hill near Centralia in 1907, including Archie Davis on horse. Below, a dozen men working for Lincoln Creek Lumber Company stand on a huge pile of logs. Lincoln Creek, northwest of Centralia, was a prime logging location. In 1903, the company built a lumber yard. In 1905, E.B. Foote and William Parks built a mill near Galvin. In 1906, William H. Thompson purchased the mill.

LEWIS COUNTY HISTORICAL MUSEUM P10966

LEWIS COUNTY HISTORICAL MUSEUM P10787

Above are the logging train tracks belonging to the Eastern Railway and Lumber Company near Centralia. At left is logging machinery belonging to the company.

LEWIS COUNTY HISTORICAL MUSEUM P10788

LEWIS COUNTY HISTORICAL MUSEUM PC1982

Above is the Lincoln Creek railroad depot on a postcard dated December 27, 1913. Below, a donkey engine on skids at an unknown logging camp, probably in Centralia, between 1910 and 1920. Among those shown are Pete Heida and A.C. Replogle.

LEWIS COUNTY HISTORICAL MUSEUM P21589

LEWIS COUNTY HISTORICAL MUSEUM P9736

Centralia saw flooding of neighborhoods in 1915. The photo above shows flooding on North King Street with the home of Willis N. Beal at far right. At left is flooding on Pine and Ash Streets.

LEWIS COUNTY HISTORICAL MUSEUM P9735

LEWIS COUNTY HISTORICAL MUSEUM P11565

The postcard above shows a birds-eye view of Centralia sometime after 1912. After the economic crash in the 1890s, Centralia rebounded and continued to grow. Below is the BPOE ELKS building decorated with flags on June 21, 1915.

LEWIS COUNTY HISTORICAL MUSEUM PC75

LEWIS COUNTY HISTORICAL MUSEUM P4796

The new Fords Prairie High School in 1916 at front with the smaller Fords Prairie Elementary School, which later became the Fords Prairie Grange Hall, in back. Below, the Centralia High School graduating class of June 5, 1916, on exterior steps. Edith L. Airron, Grace N. Arveson, Gladys E. Black, Irma V. Boatman, Earl E. Brown, Marie Christensen, Dorothy M. Clawson, Albert B. Cobb, Katherine E. Courter, Roy D. Davidson, Charles H. Eaton, Mary H. Eaton, Mary E. Everett, Ernest S. Farrell, Effie M. Fitzgerald, Myrtle M. Foron, George L. Hahn, Verle Hanna, Neva Harris, Day Hilborn, Grant Hodge, Ruth Hoss, Elmer G. Johnson, Francis Keefe, Ella M. Lammer, Margaret A, Lyness, Henry C. Madsen, Marcus O'Day, Edith Parks, George Rardin, Olivene Rhines, Aletta Rowswell, Walter Ruble, George Schacht, Ruth Schorer, Pauline Schulter, John Schummer, Ralph Smith, Boyd Thacker, Nellie Watson, Hazel Weaver, John Wheeler, George White, Camilla Williams and Blanche Workman.

LEWIS COUNTY HISTORICAL MUSEUM P6451

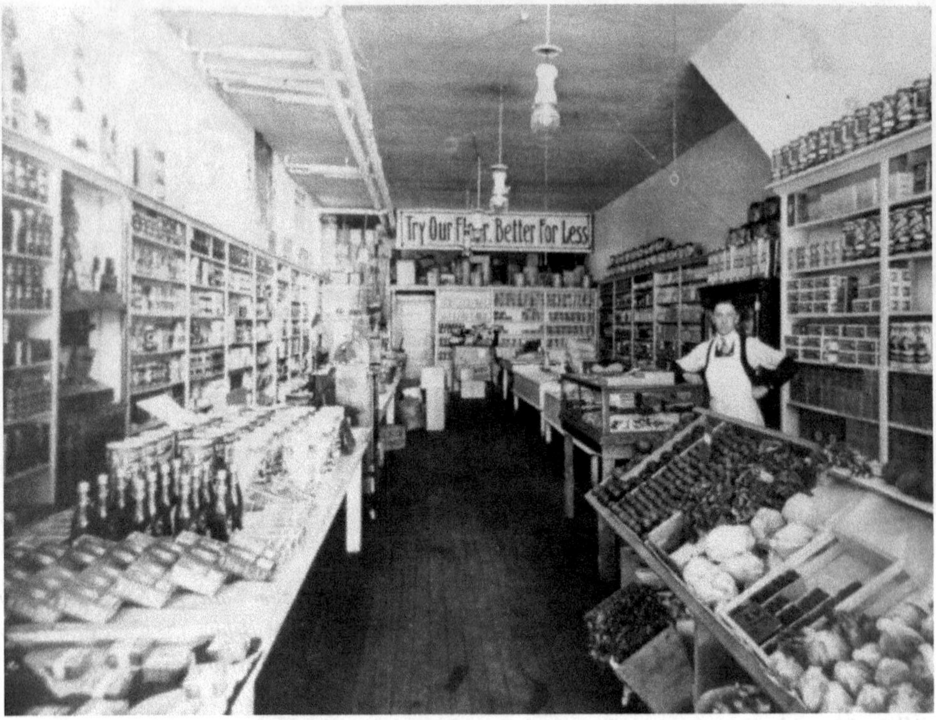

Lewis County Historical Museum P10785

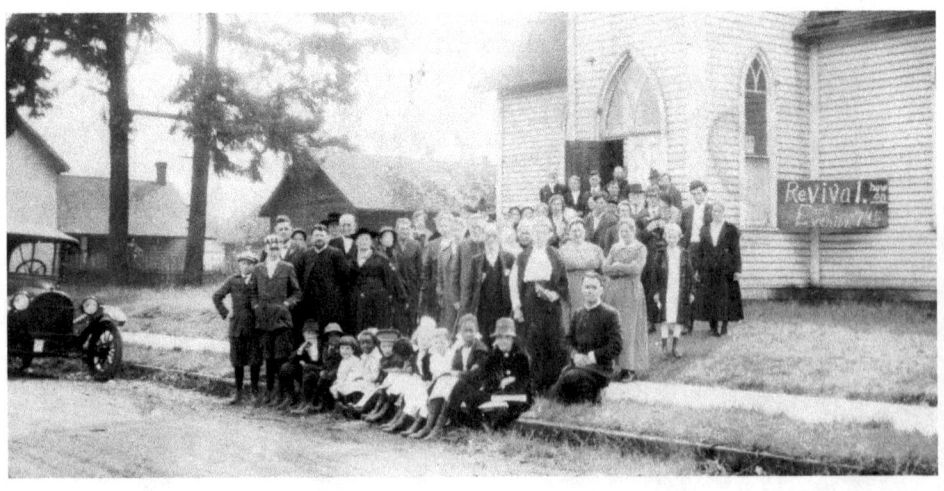

Reliance Grocery in 1919 with Clarence Helmick behind the counter. Below, a September 1919 photo of the congregation of the Church of the Brethren at Main and Gold Streets.

Lewis County Historical Museum PC1169

LEWIS COUNTY HISTORICAL MUSEUM P5184

Orville Behrbaum sits on a milk delivery truck in Centralia in 1918. He drove the truck to Mendota. Below, a troop train carrying soldiers fighting in World War I stopped at the Centralia Depot in 1918 to receive canteen meals from members of the American Red Cross.

LEWIS COUNTY HISTORICAL MUSEUM P18565

LEWIS COUNTY HISTORICAL MUSEUM P17316

The 1922 photo above shows a car on South Silver Street near the Carnegie Public Library (now Timberland Regional Library) with the first gazebo in the background. A banner on the car reads, "Centralia City Commission—20 miles paved streets." Below is a city landmark for years, the Centralia Hotel on the Pacific Highway, facing George Washington Park.

LEWIS COUNTY HISTORICAL MUSEUM PC2718

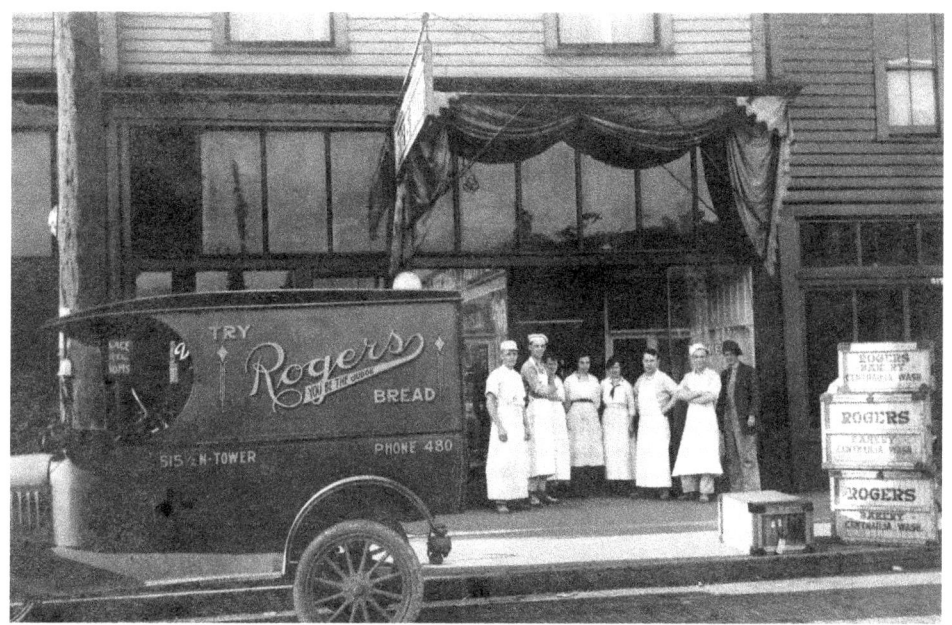

LEWIS COUNTY HISTORICAL MUSEUM P11266

Above is an undated photo of Rogers Bakery on North Tower. The Model T truck reads "Try Rogers Bread—You be the judge." Fred Adler, Sid Spaeth, unidentified women, Billie Rogers, and Henry Hankelare standing with the truck driver in front of the bakery. Below are students from either South School or Lincoln School. The teacher is at the upper right. Students' names are listed on the photo at the Lewis County Historical Museum.

LEWIS COUNTY HISTORICAL MUSEUM P451

LEWIS COUNTY HISTORICAL MUSEUM (NO ACCESSION NUMBER YET)

An early twentieth century photo of a parade in downtown Centralia.

Six

A Centralia Tragedy

The Great War raging in Europe seemed far afield until the United States joined the fight on April 6, 1917. Nearly 400 men from Centralia enlisted while others were drafted. Many Lewis County men served with Company M of the 161st Infantry, which was organized in 1910 and fought in Mexico to quell unrest south of the border in 1916.

Centralia troops sailed from New York to Europe in December. Most fought in the trenches of France; others guarded against the Bolshevik revolt in Russia and Siberia.

After the declaration of an armistice on November 11, 1918, those who didn't serve in the Army of Occupation drifted home. Many suffered the effects of mustard gas when they returned home. Others perished in the fighting of gunshots, mortars, or more frequently, the Spanish influenza that broke out in February 1918, which infected nearly a third of the world's population and killed an estimated 50 million people. Many of the 16 million who perished in World War I rest forever in graves beneath the fields of France.

On the home front, the influenza infected about 20 million among the U.S. population, killed as many as 800,000, and dropped the nation's average life expectancy by a dozen years.

Nearly as invasive as the disease lay a brewing conflict simmering beneath the surface of civility as the Industrial Workers of the World, or Wobblies, set up union headquarters in downtown Centralia, much to the consternation of city business leaders who considered them radical communists. A mob attacked Tom Lassiter, a blind man who sold pro-union newspapers in Centralia, burned his newsstand, and dumped him in a ditch in another county.

And during an American Red Cross parade on April 30, 1918, several men broke away to raid the IWW headquarters at First and B, smashed windows, and burned furniture. They hauled Wobblies into the street and beat them before dumping them outside of town with a warning not to return.

In September 1919, the Wobblies opened a new headquarters in the Roderick Hotel on North Tower Avenue.

The tensions also brought a tragedy that tainted the city for a century, a conflict between the American Legion soldiers of WWI and IWW members, or Wobblies. Some refer to it as the Centralia Massacre; others call it the Centralia Tragedy. Whatever the name, the clash in downtown Centralia killed four local WWI veterans—Warren Grimm, Arthur McElfresh, Ben Casagranda, and Dale Hubbard—after gunfire broke out on November 11, 1919, during an Armistice Day parade to celebrate the end of the Great War. That night, a mob broke into the city jail, yanked out a beaten Wobbly, Wesley Everest, and lynched him from a bridge over the Chehalis River. The Washington National Guard arrived that night to impose peace. Four days later, on November 15, 1919, a posse hunting down Wobblies accidentally shot and killed fellow civilian John Haney, a father of ten.

Nearly a dozen Wobblies, most of them Centralia residents, faced charges in the shooting death of Warren Grimm, one of the parade's leaders. With so much anger toward the Wobblies in Lewis County, a trial in 1920 was moved to Montesano, a small logging town near the Pacific coast. Charges against Bert Faulkner and Tom Morgan were dismissed, and a jury acquitted Mike Sheehan and IWW attorney Elmer Smith. Loren Roberts, initially found not guilty by reason of insanity but was declared cured after three months, spent a decade behind bars. The twelve jurors convicted eight men of second-degree murder, but a judge ignored their pleas for leniency, instead sentencing them to between twenty-five and forty years in prison.

Although disbarred, attorney Elmer Smith fought for the release of the Wobblies from prison. James McInerney died in prison in 1930. Another man was released. Three received parole in 1931. And in 1933, Governor Clarence D. Martin commuted the sentences of the remaining three. Ray Becker proclaimed his innocence and served nineteen years in prison.

For more than a century, people argued about how events unfolded on that fateful day. Did Legionnaires break formation to raid the Wobbly hall before gunshots were fired? Or were gunshots fired first, prompting the raid on the union hall?

Centralia received a visit from U.S. President Warren G. Harding on July 3, 1923, when his special train stopped for nearly an hour so he could pay tribute to the four veterans killed during the parade four years earlier. Postmaster Harry Bras drove the president in his car to visit the graves of Warren O. Grimm, Arthur McElfresh, Ben Casagranda, and Dale Hubbard with his military and naval aids and Representative Albert Johnson before returning to the train, where most of his entourage remained sleeping. Local leaders from the American Legion and the Elks greeted him. The president died less than a month later, on August 2, 1923, in San Francisco at the age of fifty-seven.

In 1924, the Legion commissioned Alonzo Victor Lewis to design The Sentinel—a bronze statue of a World War I soldier, or Doughboy—in George Washington Park to honor the four Legionnaires "slain during a peaceful parade" in their hometown. A plaque for Wesley Everest, the lynched Wobbly, was put in place at the park. In 2000, Centralia College honored IWW attorney Elmer Smith with a plaque on the Diversity Clocktower in the center of campus. And in June 2024, the Wobblies unveiled a bronze plaque in a monument near the Sentinel that bears the IWW logo and lists the "Union Victims of the Centralia Tragedy of 1919" and says seven—Eugene Barnett, Britt Smith, O.C. Bland, Bert Bland, James McInerney, John Lamb, and Loren Roberts—were incarcerated "for defending their union hall."

Although fallout from the tragedy lingered for decades, it wasn't the only time Centralia made headlines in the early part of the twentieth century. In 1921, Centralia Police Officer Louis Sonney, who had previously worked in the Tono coal mines, captured a notorious yet charming train robber, Roy Gardner, known as the smiling bandit. While traveling to the federal penitentiary at McNeil Island, Gardner escaped from a train and the two U.S. marshals transporting him while in Castle Rock. He covered his face with bandages to conceal his identity, telling the Oxford Hotel staff he had been severely burned, but the proprietor, Gertrude Howell, and Officer Sonney grew suspicious, and Sonney arrested him. The criminal known as an escape artist later was incarcerated at Alcatraz. Sonney's son, Dan, produced a documentary in 2001 recounting the arrest and his father's switch to producing B movies in Hollywood.

The Armistice Day tragedy received renewed interest nearly eighty years later with the unveiling in 1997 of a controversial two-story mural, "The Resurrection of Wesley Everest," painted on the Centralia Square Antique Mall.

Labor muralist Mike Alewitz, a Central Connecticut State University professor, painted the mural, which was thirty feet wide and twenty-five feet high. It featured Wesley Everest as a martyr at the center with union activists guarding the IWW hall. It featured blind newsstand owner Tom Lassiter who was run out of town before the tragedy, and black cats, a symbol for sabotage, raining down on the capitalist town with a steam plant and coal mining in the background. It also depicts IWW workers with banners, a pie in the sky reference to a hymn with wet angels—the wives of Wobblies—holding a sign after being doused with fire hoses. The artist depicted a man in a suit, whom he described as an ugly human, spewing fecal matter from his mouth that turned into a mob of people with crosses, nooses, and American flags marching on the Wobbly hall. Lumber barons depicted as a capitalist pig are seen surrounded by trees and bags of money. Elks members were seen as rats with a noose, knife, and gun.

LEWIS COUNTY HISTORICAL MUSEUM P11568

The peaceful town of Centralia erupted into violence on November 11, 1919. Above is Main Street looking west with two cars parked on left side of street.

LEWIS COUNTY HISTORICAL MUSEUM P8667

This undated photo shows Wesley Everest on the right, working on cutting down a tree with another logger.

When the parade stopped to reform in front of the Roderick Hotel on North Tower, headquarters of the Industrial Workers of the World, some say a faction of veterans broke off to raid the hall and Wobblies fired back to defend themselves. Others says the Wobblies fired before the raid took place.

LEWIS COUNTY HISTORICAL MUSEUM P10989

LEWIS COUNTY HISTORICAL MUSEUM P4428

The Armistice Day parade on November 11, 1919, started out peacefullly as seen above in this photo. When gunfire broke out, killing and wounding WWI veterans, police officers incarcerated members of the Industrial Workers of the World in the city jail, seen below. In 1919 the jail stood at the site where the City Hall is now. In this photo, from an old pamphlet on the Armistice Day Tragedy of 1919, men are carrying the body of Wesley Everest from the jail to a van that took it to the Greenwood Cemetery in Centralia for burial. After Everest was lynched, his body was taken to the jail and left there for two days prior to burial.

LEWIS COUNTY HISTORICAL MUSEUM P8666

LEWIS COUNTY HISTORICAL MUSEUM P14398

The four World War I veterans marching with the American Legion who died as a result of the Armistice Day parade were, from left, Ernest Dale Hubbard, Warren O. Grimm at top, Arthur McElfresh at right, and Ben Casagranda at the bottom. One of the men injured in the shooting was Eugene Fitzer, seen here in October 1917 in his Company M uniform. He was shot in his left wrist, and the bullet exited through his elbow.

LEWIS COUNTY HISTORICAL MUSEUM P3441

LEWIS COUNTY HISTORICAL MUSEUM P14033

The front page of the November 11, 1919, issue of The Centralia Daily Chronicle. *One headline reads, "McElfresh, Grimm and Casagranda Killed by I. W. W." Dale Hubbard died later.*

LEWIS COUNTY HISTORICAL MUSEUM P17795

LEWIS COUNTY HISTORICAL MUSEUM P14400

A mob broke into the city jail and pulled out Wesley Everest (pictured on left), an IWW activist who was beaten before being jailed. They lynched him from the Mellen Street bridge (pictured above) on the night of November 11, 1919. He was buried in Sticklin Greenwood Cemetery.

LEWIS COUNTY HISTORICAL MUSEUM P10959

NATIONAL GUARD PHOTO ON WIKIMEDIA COMMONS

Above, residents gather for the funeral of Ben Casagranda, one of the veterans killed during the Armistice Day parade. At left is a National Guard photo of the burial of Wesley Everest after his lynching. Below is the grave of Wesley Everest.

LEWIS COUNTY HISTORICAL MUSEUM P1542

LEWIS COUNTY HISTORICAL MUSEUM P15890

This 1921 photo shows the seven convicted IWW men at Walla Walla, Washington. In the back, from left, are Ray Becker, O.C. Bland, Britt Smith, and Bert Bland. In the front, from left, are Eugene Barnett, John Lamb, and James McInerney. Although the jury recommended leniency, the judge sentenced them to decades in prison. Attorney Elmer Smith fought for and eventually secured their release. In the mid-1920s, the American Legion erected a statue of a WWI Doughboy, seen at right, with side panels showing the images of the four men killed during the parade. The words "peaceful parade" rankled union activists and others who insisted the veterans planned an attack on the Wobbly Hall.

LEWIS COUNTY HISTORICAL MUSEUM 2667

LEWIS COUNTY HISTORICAL MUSEUM P14401

Citizens gather near The Sentinel statue at Washington Park in this undated photo. Below is a controversial mural painted across the street in the 1990s. At left, the IWW finally succeeded in 2023 in erecting a bronze plaque in the park to honor 'union victims' of the tragedy.

PHOTO COURTESY OF *THE CHRONICLE*

AUTHOR PHOTO

LEWIS COUNTY HISTORICAL MUSEUM P9670

Women marching in a July 5, 1920, parade photographed at the corner of Main and Pearl Streets. The police department and Schaht & Heampe can be seen in the background. Below is the Thompson-Hackney home in Centralia, which was built in 1908. The home on North Pearl and First Street was later owned by Lorraine Williams in the 1980s.

LEWIS COUNTY HISTORICAL MUSEUM P10932

LEWIS COUNTY HISTORICAL MUSEUM P17353

The photo above, likely from the 1920s, shows Polar Ice Cream Company employees on North Tower Avenue after its expansion by manager J. A. Winchell. Below, people gather for the Women Educators Home Products Exhibit at George Washington Park in June 1921.

LEWIS COUNTY HISTORICAL MUSEUM P988

LEWIS COUNTY HISTORICAL MUSEUM P994

A First Guaranty Bank employee works during its opening on August 31, 1921. Albert Smith bought the Field and Lease Bank around 1918, renaming it to First Guaranty Bank. Below, is a photo of the Washington Hotel on the corner of Third and North Tower in 1921. From 1921 to 1928, Belle Garland, grandmother of Mary Lorsung, owned the hotel.

LEWIS COUNTY HISTORICAL MUSEUM P4429

LEWIS COUNTY HISTORICAL MUSEUM P16997

The Centralia Millwork and Supply Company burns on June 11, 1921. Fires were a somewhat common occurrence in mills and other buildings in the early twentieth century. Below, the 1922 class photo of second-graders on the steps of Fords Prairie School. The teacher was Myrtle Foran.

LEWIS COUNTY HISTORICAL MUSEUM P6091

The photo at left shows the Liberty Theatre and Liberty Drug Company on Tower Avenue and Center Street during one of the major floods, probably the one in 1933. Below, workers for Lincoln Creek Lumber Company and their dog gather in front of a logging steam engine in 1925.

LEWIS COUNTY HISTORICAL MUSEUM P15291

LEWIS COUNTY HISTORICAL MUSEUM P10790

LEWIS COUNTY HISTORICAL MUSEUM P1000

The First Guaranty Bank at the corner of Tower and Main Street in about 1925. Below, a look inside the bank in 1922.

LEWIS COUNTY HISTORICAL MUSEUM P1014

LEWIS COUNTY HISTORICAL MUSEUM P17330

The Health Institute Building on corner of two unknown streets, likely in Centralia, with three early 1920s touring cars parked at curb. Below is a photo of the Centralia General Hospital, which was built around 1923 on South Gold Street and later served as the Peter Pan Nursing Home in the 1970s and 1980s, a homeless shelter, and since 1998, business offices.

LEWIS COUNTY HISTORICAL MUSEUM P15341

LEWIS COUNTY HISTORICAL MUSEUM P19218

Luther Rigg on the left in the photo above with early sound car, an open touring sedan with a standing sign on top advertising sound systems and a motor specialty garage. It also has a spare wheel cover with an ad for Centralia Pioneer Days Celebration August 4th through 6th. On the far side of the car, the man with the pipe is Milt Jastram, police chief, and on left front is Jim Kendricks, a radio repairman. Below is the Sweet Clinic private hospital, later St. Luke's.

LEWIS COUNTY HISTORICAL MUSEUM P11632

Seven

GHOST TOWNS

Development in the early part of the twentieth century brought immigrants flocking to Centralia and outlying communities to work in coal mines, sawmills, and log the abundant forests.

Large coal mines sprang up in the early 1900s. The Wilson Coal Company opened at Kopiah northeast of Centralia in 1906 and shipped 46,000 tons the first year, while the Miller Brothers and later Superior Mine and Sheldon Mine operated near Coal Creek between Centralia and Chehalis. Another mine opened on Fords Prairie northwest of Centralia, operating from 1911 to 1934, when fired forced its closure. It reopened as Monarch Mine, which had previously operated in the Little Hanaford Valley. The Black Prairie Mine opened in 1929 in the Big Hanaford Valley eight miles northeast of Centralia, taking over the Victory Coal Mining Company after it closed in 1925. Martin Coal Mining Company opened in 1932 but struggled with a lack of markets for coal. Jay Cribble operated Lincoln Creek Mine. Puget Sound Power and Light had Coal Creek Mine.

Two of these mines led to creation of communities that later became ghost towns.

In June 1907, the Washington Union Coal Company, a subsidiary of the Union Pacific Railroad, started the town of Tono about eleven miles northeast of Centralia. European immigrants built new lives while working in Tono after leaving homes in Finland, England, Italy, Czechoslovakia, and other nations.

Within a decade, the community boasted a population of nearly one thousand people. Residents lived in a hundred company houses, each encircled by a white picket fence, and cooked on woodstoves. They had no water or electricity and used outhouses during the day and chamber pots at night.

Men could stand rather than kneel in tunnels as they worked ten hours a day in the open-pit mine known as the Hanaford Big Seam. They dug holes in the soft coal using seven-foot-long hand drills or augers for dynamite to find narrow veins, then dug coal from the mine, working in damp and dusty conditions with wages dependent on how much coal they dug each day. They loaded coal into small containers, which mules hauled from the mine on tracks until the company installed an electric winch in the mid-1920s. Two men working together could remove nearly ten tons of coal in a day, according to an article in *The Daily Chronicle*. The daily output averaged 1,200 tons a day in the mine, considered one of the Northwest's safest.

By the mid-1920s, the town of Tono had two hundred houses, a hospital, a women's clubhouse, stores, and a public school. Residents purchased goods at the company store using script or a charge account and settled their tabs on payday. The community even fielded a baseball team with cheerleaders.

But demand for coal dropped in 1932 when the Union Pacific switched to fueling locomotives with oil, and the town began to die until it faded away to a valley filled with fir trees.

Another town opened up northeast of Centralia in the Packwood Creek Valley, named for William "Billy" Packwood who homesteaded and farmed in the area in 1883. Then Bernard Hawley Johnston discovered a vein of coal across from his new homestead. In October 1907, he incorporated the Mendota Coal and Coke Company, naming it for his Missouri hometown. He built the Centralia Eastern Railroad spur line from the mine to provide coal to the nearby Northern Pacific Company as fuel for its locomotives. The company leased more than 9,000 acres for mining.

The town of Mendota grew to include sixty-five rental homes, a three-story hotel, a general company store, a post office, a train depot, and a one-room school on a hill that served students in first through eighth grades. It later expanded to two rooms and served as a home, a Saturday evening dance hall, and a place to meet on the following morning for church and Sunday school taught by a woman from the Salvation Army, which served Doughboys free coffee and donuts during World War I. The school also served as a gathering place for checker tournaments and card parties. Residents drew water for cooking from hydrants every four houses or so and drinking water from a well in the town's center, but Mendota was a "dry" town with no saloons allowed to open there.

During its heyday, the Mendota company employed as many as two hundred men who earned an average of $3.50 a day for working eight hours, six days a week. The schoolteacher received about eighty dollars a month. Monthly rent for a three-room house, often shared by two families, was between eight and twelve dollars. The Olympic Mine also operated near Mendota from 1918 until 1925.

In 1921, about the time power lines arrived at Mendota, labor rumblings surfaced with wildcat strikes unauthorized by union leadership and a lawsuit filed by a neighbor against the Mendota Coal and Coke management. The school shut down, and students were bused elsewhere.

An underground fire in 1926 destroyed much of mine, which closed its operations. The town gradually disappeared, the buildings abandoned and falling into ruins, the land replaced by a sheep ranch. By the 1950s, Mendota remained only a memory listed occasionally as one of many long-gone ghost towns.

LEWIS COUNTY HISTORICAL MUSEUM P4358

An early 1900s elevated view of Tono with houses in the foreground and the mine in the background.

LEWIS COUNTY HISTORICAL MUSEUM P10528

Tono miner Richard Thompson in the 1930s.

LEWIS COUNTY HISTORICAL MUSEUM P12349

The 1908 photo above shows the coal mine tipple at Tono with women and children pictured. At left, the 1900 photo of the entrance of the Tono mine above bears a warning sign that reads, "Danger—Keep off slope."

LEWIS COUNTY HISTORICAL MUSEUM P4852

Tono miners at the mine tipple, circa 1907.

Lewis County Historical Museum P4055

LEWIS COUNTY HISTORICAL MUSEUM P12811

A September 29, 1927, photo of the Northern Pacific Railroad at Wabash north of Hanaford Creek, looking south. Below, a photo from the 1910s of the town of Mendota, Washington, shows a clearcut, sawmills, railroad tracks, and houses. The tall building on the right may have been a boarding house.

LEWIS COUNTY HISTORICAL MUSEUM P2436

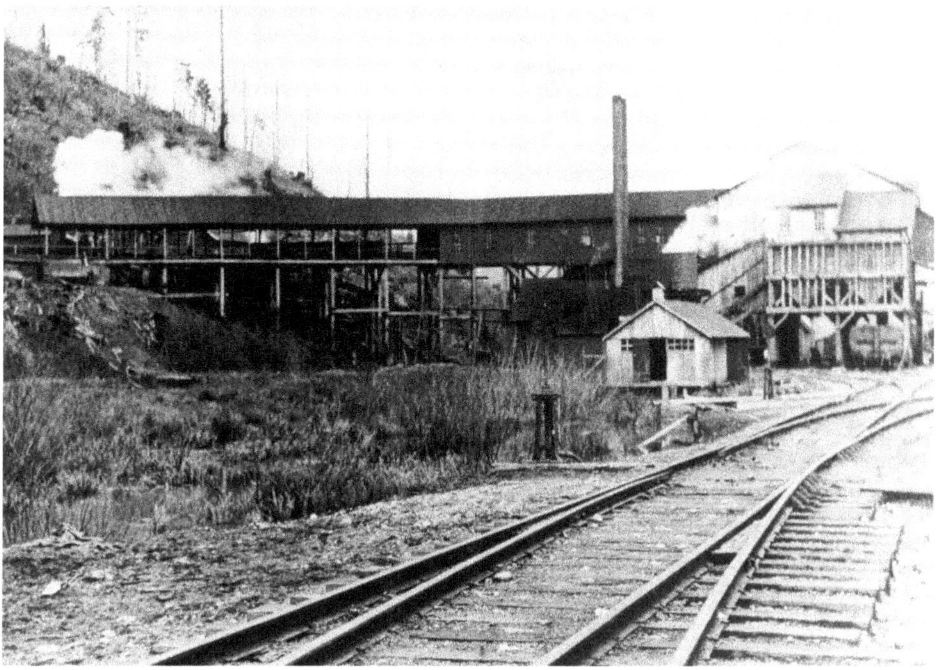

The photo above shows the Eastern Railway and Lumber Company mill at Mendotain 1914 or 1915, while the one below shows it in 1918.

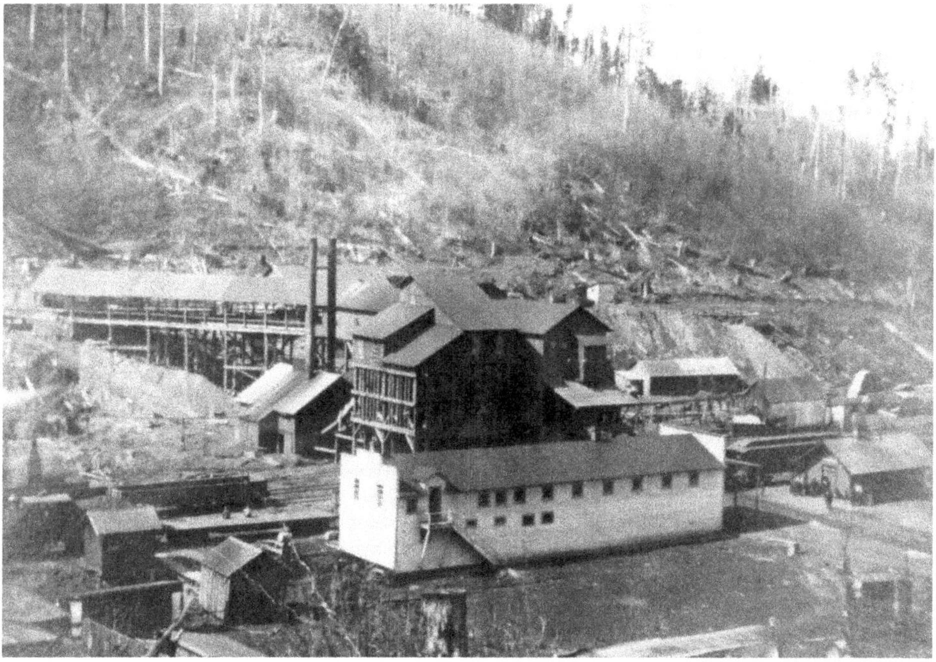

LEWIS COUNTY HISTORICAL MUSEUM P4235

The undated photo above shows men in front of the work hall in Mendota. Below, the town of Mendota in 1914. The town provided jobs for loggers, sawmill workers, and miners. Little sign of the community remains today.

LEWIS COUNTY HISTORICAL MUSEUM P4236

LEWIS COUNTY HISTORICAL MUSEUM P5190

These 1918 photos from Orville Behrbaum show the mine at Mendota, including a closeup of the mine site with the powder house far right and center. The rail lines pass directly by the mine. At lower left is a crude log cabin on a hill overlooking Mendota. Children used it as a clubhouse. At lower right is the powder house with smoke behind it from a large mine fire.

LEWIS COUNTY HISTORICAL MUSEUM P5189

LEWIS COUNTY HISTORICAL MUSEUM P5196

LEWIS COUNTY HISTORICAL MUSEUM P5202

Above is an undated photo of miners at entrance to the Mendota mine. At left in 1900 is the Mendota Mine Safety Crew.

LEWIS COUNTY HISTORICAL MUSEUM P6956

LEWIS COUNTY HISTORICAL MUSEUM P12270

Seven men sit on and around a ten-foot-high old growth stump with houses on either side, likely in Mendota about 1910. Below, a 1910 photo shows an Eastern Railway and Lumber Company crew at Mendota.

LEWIS COUNTY HISTORICAL MUSEUM P18796

165

LEWIS COUNTY HISTORICAL MUSEUM P8264

The undated photo above shows the Mendota Mining Company Mine Tipple. Below, the photo from August 7, 1928, shows the Northern Pacific Railroad at Wabash, looking north.

LEWIS COUNTY HISTORICAL MUSEUM P12810

Eight

A College, Depression, and War

As logging and mining faded from the local economy, stalwart educators at Centralia High School envisioned a future where students could continue their education at home.

In 1925, two years after accepting a job as Centralia's school superintendent, Nebraska native Charles Lester "C.L." Littel, aided by Miss Margaret Corbet, an English teacher born in Northern Ireland, opened a junior college on the third floor of the relatively new $40,000 high school, which had opened in 1912 in a block bordered by Pear, Iron, Walnut and Rock streets.

Corbet, the college's first principal or dean who held that post for twenty-five years, continued to teach both high school and college students. College enrollment grew during the first five years to 141 in 1930, and tuition cost thirty-five dollars a quarter, or $110 per year. The two dozen graduates could transfer to any higher education institute that accepted University of Washington credits. In 1932, Miss Katharine Kemp, a Michigan native who grew up in Idaho, joined the junior college staff teaching languages, psychology, and business, and served thirty-seven years as dean of women.

The late 1920s and early 1930s saw continued growth in Centralia, with the opening in 1926 of the elegant and luxurious 105-room Lewis and Clark Hotel at 117 West Magnolia, the city's tallest building. It featured a huge lobby with marble floors and elaborate chandeliers dangling from the ceilings, a 1,500-square-foot ballroom with hardwood floors, and a 1,200-square-foot banquet room.

The same year The Aerie opened at 219 South Tower Avenue with a 5,000-plus-square-foot event grand ballroom, banquet and café space, and antique cherry-wood bar from the 1800s. The Eagles fraternal organization leased the first floor to Spike Motor Company, Busek's Creamery, and Martin Motor Parts and later the Centralia Beauty College.

The city thrummed with excitement with the opening of the iconic golden-toned art deco three-level Fox Theatre at 119 South Tower Avenue on September 10, 1930. The $200,000 theater, part of the Fox West Coast Theatre chain and the largest theater between Portland and Tacoma, featured plush carpet, 1,200 seats, a full-size pipe organ, and elaborate ceiling lights.

Then the Great Depression devastated the nation's economy. The stock market crashed. Stores shut down. Banks closed, and the city was without a financial institution for seven months. Citizens pitched in to create a relief fund to help destitute families. Businesses donated bread, milk, coal, wood, shoes, and furniture for neighbors in need. The Works Progress Administration put eighty unemployed men to work for fifty cents an hour, six days a week, improving the fairgrounds, building playgrounds, fixing dams, and improving Borst Park, the airport, the library, city parks, and streets.

People stayed home, played cards and checkers, pitched horseshoes, or occasionally scraped together fifty cents for admission to the newly opened Fox Theatre. Citizens organized its first Pioneer Days celebration at the park in August 1931, replacing the Pioneer Picnic that started in 1912. Men, women, and children dressed in pioneer costumes for a parade to honor the settlers who founded the community.

Enrollment plummeted at Centralia Junior College to fewer than sixty as more young people worked to help their families and couldn't afford the time or tuition, even though the college accepted promissory notes from students. Teachers agreed to accept less cash for salaries, accepting bank notes for partial payment. But when the banks closed, Corbet asked teachers for the least amount they could live on each month. Businesses offered five, ten, or twenty dollars a month to keep the college operating. By 1936, the faculty received back pay and sixty-two guarantors saw their contributions repaid. By 1939, enrollment had returned to 145, and more than 300 students had graduated from the college during its first fourteen years.

The brick post office building with decorative flourishes across from George Washington Park was constructed in 1937.

But then the Japanese attacked Pearl Harbor on December 7, 1941, and the United States joined World War II. Enrollment plunged again from 148 to only twenty-nine freshmen and three sophomores in the 1945 graduating class as men enlisted, and women found jobs in defense industries to help the war effort. Teachers and students joined the military to fight for freedom. The college provided training programs for pilots, radio technicians, and others to help the war effort. Students and staff collected materials for recycling, bought war stamps and bonds, donated blood, worked with the Red Cross to make bandages, and staffed an observation post on campus at Noble Field to search for enemy aircraft. Women joined the United Service Organization to keep soldiers entertained while on leave. Despite the lower enrollment, Corbet and Kemp did what they could to keep the doors open.

The end of World War II brought a surge in college enrollment to 242 by 1948 as returning soldiers used the GI bill to continue their interrupted education. The overcrowded third floor of the high school no longer sufficed as a junior college, so classes were held in the former Free Methodist Church and two temporary government surplus buildings.

Then, on April 13, 1949, at 11:55 a.m., an earthquake measuring 7.1 on the Richter scale shook Western Washington communities for up to forty-five seconds. Bricks toppled from buildings, crushing to death a sixty-nine-year-old Centralia man on Tower Avenue, the eighteen-year-old Castle Rock High School senior class president, an eleven-year-old crossing guard in Tacoma, and a pipefitter at an Olympia veneer plant. Four others died in the quake centered at Littlerock north of Centralia, which caused an estimated $100 million in damage regionally.

Centralia dismissed classes for spring break to inspect schools for damage from the earthquake, which led to condemnation of Washington School. The district tore down Logan School, too, and erected new schools at both sites. The district also set aside money for a college center, which opened in the fall of 1950. The 50,000-square-foot brick-and-tile building was in the 600 block of West Locust.

A century after its humble beginning, Centralia College, the oldest continuously operating community college in Washington State, covers more than thirty beautifully landscaped acres with a dozen buildings and offers applied bachelor's degrees in applied management, behavioral healthcare, diesel technology, software engineering, and kindergarten-to-eighth-grade teacher education.

Adna artist Jim Stafford, who taught at Centralia College, created a life-size bronze statue of Corbet and Kemp, which was unveiled in the center of campus in June 2014. It bears the words the two women took to heart during World War II to "keep the doors open." They did.

Local rivers overflowed their banks several times during the early twentieth century, resulting in floods throughout Centralia and Lewis County. City leaders worried after a 1919 flood that the old Fort Borst blockhouse would be swept away, so they moved it to its present location in Fort Borst Park. In December 1921, China Creek and the Skookumchuck River overflowed, flooding cellars and basements of homes and stores. A dozen years later, in December 1933, rain pummeled the region, dumping more than 22 inches of the year's total 59 inches. It still stands as Centralia's wettest month on record.

Heavy rain hit the area again in 1936, 1937, 1946, and in the spring of 1948, flooding on the Columbia River wiped out the community of Vanport near Portland.

LEWIS COUNTY HISTORICAL MUSEUM P16177

Mary Elizabeth Crum Brunton and her uncle Ed Kennedy in an automobile on Waunch Prairie in 1910.

LEWIS COUNTY HISTORICAL MUSEUM P7588

People stand on the sidewalk of West Pine Street in Centralia about 1920 watching a toppled World War I Army tank used after the fighting to knock down houses to be razed around the city. In background is the Edward Newell Undertaking at 205 W. Pine. To the right is the First Baptist Church, which burned in the early 1920s, replaced by a brick building on the same foundation in 1925. The brick building, badly cracked in 1949 earthquake, was later covered in stucco. In 1965 the church erected a new building at 930 N. Scheuber Road, and Newell-Hoerling Mortuary purchased the building. Below, a Lincoln Creek Lumber donkey and crew between Bunker Creek and Lincoln Creek about 1928.

LEWIS COUNTY HISTORICAL MUSEUM P9982

LEWIS COUNTY HISTORICAL MUSEUM P12273

Members of the Eastern Railway crew, one holding a dog, stand on a steam engine platform east of Centralia around the early 1900s. Below, four men stand on top of a log near Lincoln Creek around 1928. These men were part of the Schafer Brothers Logging Company.

LEWIS COUNTY HISTORICAL MUSEUM P9983

LEWIS COUNTY HISTORICAL MUSEUM P4999

In the 1929 photo above, Lincoln Creek Lumber Company workers pose on logs. The photo was taken between Bunker Creek and Lincoln Creek. Below, a reprint from Del Olsen's glass plates shows the railway switching station just north of Centralia as seen from the top of the old wooden viaduct that crossed railroad tracks at Fifth Street sometime before 1930 when the new Sixth Street viaduct was built. At left are the switch yard, the Ward Blue and Daviscourt Evergreen business building, the water tower, and coal bunkers in front of the roundhouse. At center is the Western Mill with houses on the right facing Delaware Street.

LEWIS COUNTY HISTORICAL MUSEUM P2271

LEWIS COUNTY HISTORICAL MUSEUM P21585

A single Douglas fir loaded on a railroad flat car at Centralia. No identification of the man in the photo. The photo below is labeled "Centralia Saw Mill." Lumber mills were a huge source of economic development for Centralia and the surrounding areas in the early settlement days.

LEWIS COUNTY HISTORICAL MUSEUM PC2722

LEWIS COUNTY HISTORICAL MUSEUM P12521

LEWIS COUNTY HISTORICAL MUSEUM P17336

The Agnew Lumber Company—later just the Agnew Company—bought Eastern Railway and Lumber Company assets. Sam Agnew worked for Eastern Railway, owned stock, and oversaw operations as general manager. Two years after fire destroyed the Eastern mill, Sam and his son, Jay, formed S.A. Agnew Lumber Company and began operations in 1941. At its peak, Agnew employed about four hundred but closed in 1959. At left is Woolworths 5-10 and 15 Cent Store in the Landers Building at 209 N. Tower. A hotel opened on the second floor in July 1912 and operated until 1929–30.

LEWIS COUNTY HISTORICAL MUSEUM P11578

The 1926 photo in front of the old fire station shows a firetruck rebuilt using parts from a 1911 truck. Below, also in 1926, as a fundraiser, the Fraternal Order of Eagles Aerie 512 sold five shares for fifty cents for a chance to win the Chrysler sedan.

LEWIS COUNTY HISTORICAL MUSEUM P15377

LEWIS COUNTY HISTORICAL MUSEUM P11613

These undated photos show Hub City Transfer and Storage vehicles, above, and Reid Conrad, the owner of the business, inside the office. He stands behind a large counter by the telephone.

LEWIS COUNTY HISTORICAL MUSEUM P11612

LEWIS COUNTY HISTORICAL MUSEUM P11594

LEWIS COUNTY HISTORICAL MUSEUM P1091

Like the Centralia Hotel, the Lewis and Clark Hotel on North Pearl Street soon became a landmark in the city. Above are two photos showing the exterior of the hotel, the one at left from 1927. Below is an undated phtoo of the lobby inside.

LEWIS COUNTY HISTORICAL MUSEUM P11582

LEWIS COUNTY HISTORICAL MUSEUM P17360

On May 22, 1926, the Nazarene North Pacific Assembly gathered at the Centralia Elks building on Locust Street. Below is a photo from around 1931 or 1932 of the Church of the Nazarene on North Tower. Between 1922 and 1946, the church resided here. Then, in the early 1960s, construction began on the new church on West First Street, completed in 1963.

LEWIS COUNTY HISTORICAL MUSEUM P15380

LEWIS COUNTY HISTORICAL MUSEUM P11677

This 1926 photo shows Centralia General Hospital. Below in this 1940 photo is St. Luke's Hospital, which was across from Edison School on First Street.

LEWIS COUNTY HISTORICAL MUSEUM P6363

In 1925, educator Margaret Corbet worked with C.L. Littel, public school superintendent, to establish a junior college on the third floor of the high school building, seen below. Corbet and teacher and women's dean Katharine Kemp kept the doors open through the Depression and World War II, despite dwindling resources and student enrollment. At left is Robert Neal, an artist who painted a portrait of Margaret Corbet in 1980.

LEWIS COUNTY HISTORICAL MUSEUM P7587

LEWIS COUNTY HISTORICAL MUSEUM P21574

LEWIS COUNTY HISTORICAL MUSEUM P16551

On March 29, 1935, the Centralia Junior College drama class performed "Pirates with a Past." The audience watched the production in the Centralia High School auditorium, below. The view below shows the main floor and the gallery. The auditorium could seat 800, with 575 on the main floor and 225 in the gallery.

LEWIS COUNTY HISTORICAL MUSEUM P4648

Lewis County Historical Museum P4689

As the number of students increased after World War II, the junior college finally obtained its own building in 1950 with the opening of Kemp Hall, seen above in its early years and below in 1966. The college has seen enrollment increase from fifteen initially to more than four thousand. It also offers four-year bachelor's degrees in specific areas of study.

Lewis County Historical Museum P7945

LEWIS COUNTY HISTORICAL MUSEUM P8370

The new high school and college gynmansium was completed in the mid-1930s. The college renovated the gymnasium and, in 2008, opened the Health and Wellness Center, which includes classrooms, training rooms, and the gymnasium, which was dedicated to Michael D. Smith and Family. The court was dedicated in 2013 as Watterson Court.

AUTHOR PHOTO

AUTHOR PHOTO

The campus welcomes visitors with the stone marker above. In recent years, the college constructed the Walton Science Center, Washington Hall with its 500-seat Corbet Theater, and the TransAlta Commons. A bronze statue on campus by Adna artist Jim Stafford depicts Corbet and Kemp with the admonishment to "keep the doors open."

AUTHOR PHOTO

LEWIS COUNTY HISTORICAL MUSEUM P3074

The past met the future at Centralia College in 1976 when Chehalis native Hazel Pete taught basket weaving to young and old. At right, Adna artist Jim Stafford stands near the bronze statue he created of Margaret Corbet and Katharine Kemp. Its title is "Keep the Doors Open." The statue was dedicated in June 2014.

AUTHOR PHOTO

The 1997 Centralia College Clock Tower welcomes people to the campus and celebrates diversity with panels honoring Northwest individuals and groups who have made significant contributions to the history, community, or culture.

AUTHOR PHOTO

LEWIS COUNTY HISTORICAL MUSEUM P9918

A view in the early 1930s of the corner of West Main and Tower Avenue. The sign designating Centralia as 'Hub City' hangs above the intersection. Streets are lined with 1920s and 1930s cars. Below are 1930 photos of the Centralia Fire Station at the corner of Maple and Pearl Streets.

LEWIS COUNTY HISTORICAL MUSEUM P11576

LEWIS COUNTY HISTORICAL MUSEUM P1165

LEWIS COUNTY HISTORICAL MUSEUM P17320

In 1926, the English Lutheran Church on North Oak gathered for the seventh annual Pacific District of Luther League convention. A sign on the building reads, "Welcome Luther Leaguers." Below, from the book, History of Centralia Saint Mary's Catholic Church, 1910-86, *is a photo of the church's interior about 1910.*

LEWIS COUNTY HISTORICAL MUSEUM P8263

LEWIS COUNTY HISTORICAL MUSEUM PC197

Above, a crowd gathered downtown on Magnolia and Tower in Centralia for the 1933 Pioneer Day Parade. The Proffitt Building, First National Bank, and Dysart and Ellsbury Law Office are shown. Below is an early airplane and pilot, tentatively identified as Claude Berlin of Centralia, probably at Borst Park airport in the late 1920s or early 1930s before it closed.

LEWIS COUNTY HISTORICAL MUSEUM P

LEWIS COUNTY HISTORICAL MUSEUM P15381

During the early 1930s, in the midst of the Great Depression, a string band offers hope and entertainment outside The Salvation Army building on South Tower. The building housed The Salvation Army from 1925 until the late 1940s, when it moved to Rose Street. In 1990, it moved again on North Gold Street. Below, flooding from China Creek in 1933 inundated the street near Eubanks and Matthew's Machine Shop.

LEWIS COUNTY HISTORICAL MUSEUM P11639

LEWIS COUNTY HISTORICAL MUSEUM P15094

During the December 10, 1933, flood, water flowed over North Tower from the Skookumchuck River, flooding Bassett's Home Cooked Food and Liberty Theatre on the left as well as the Pacific Hotel, Lenox Hotel, Centralia Photo Shop, and Walker Paint Company on the right as well as other businesses seen in the photo below.

LEWIS COUNTY HISTORICAL MUSEUM P15095

Lewis County Historical Museum PC2187

Centralia's new post office opened on July 1, 1937, and about 1,500 people attended the official open house. Planning for the $96,000 building started in 1931, and a $6,500 site was selected in 1935. Architect Louis A. Simon designed the red brick building, which used Tenino sandstone for detail work. Harry Boyer and Sons of Olympia served as general contractor. The Works Progress Administration completed the post office, armory, gymnasium, and other projects in the city. Below is an undated sign on a building that reads, "Bungalow Lunch Meals" for twenty-five cents and hamburgers for ten or fifteen cents. The Bungalow Restaurant, owned by John Millman and Marian Bullock on South Tower, survived the Great Depression.

Lewis County Historical Museum P8567

LEWIS COUNTY HISTORICAL MUSEUM PC2371

The top photo shows the Eastern Railway and Lumber Company mill on fire in Centralia on August 6, 1939. This fire destroyed the mill completely, shutting down operations. Below is the bank building on the corner of Main and Tower in Centralia about 1935. Upstairs are the offices of attorney William H. Cameron and Van D. Timmerman Real Estate. The sign at left says, "Eat with Art and Bill."

LEWIS COUNTY HISTORICAL MUSEUM P18973

At left, the daughter of Mr. and Mrs. W.A. Raymond stands on the cow-catcher of a railroad engine near the Centralia Union Depot in October 1936. Below, a man stands in front of a large log on a flatbed truck at the Centralia depot. The inscription says, "Giant Douglas Fir From Lewis County, Wash. 11 Feet Diam.—Cut July 1939."

LEWIS COUNTY HISTORICAL MUSEUM P18017

LEWIS COUNTY HISTORICAL MUSEUM P4393

LEWIS COUNTY HISTORICAL MUSEUM P18177

A tank stops in front of the old Farmers and Merchants Bank building in 1940, when the building housed the National Bank of Commerce. The photo caption says, "Money Convoy From National Bank of Commerce, Centralia, WA." Below, on August 5, 1940, a group of men from Company C gather at the Centralia Union Depot.

LEWIS COUNTY HISTORICAL MUSEUM P13526

LEWIS COUNTY HISTORICAL MUSEUM P18173

An overview of Centralia from Seminary Hill shows the Elks building at the mid-left side, the railroad depot at the center right side, and a clump of trees at city park. The tall white building above the depot is the Centralia General Hospital built in 1926. Below, standing in front of the 1921 City Hall and police and fire stations in the late 1940s are, from left, Vernon Fear, J.E. Raught, Police Chief Rucker, and Mayor Oscar Nelson.

LEWIS COUNTY HISTORICAL MUSEUM P2973

LEWIS COUNTY HISTORICAL MUSEUM P3617

In 1943, the Washington State National Guard trained in Centralia, using the Elks building and the Centralia Armory to prepare for fighting overseas during World War II. Below, they eat at the Centralia Armory.

LEWIS COUNTY HISTORICAL MUSEUM P3623

LEWIS COUNTY HISTORICAL MUSEUM P3624

Training to look for enemies, the Washington State National Guard practiced in Centralia, the Elks building, the Centralia Armory, George Washington Park, and even Borst Park during their time in the city in 1943.

LEWIS COUNTY HISTORICAL MUSEUM P3628

LEWIS COUNTY HISTORICAL MUSEUM P3618

The Washington State National Guard's Company L, 3rd Battalion, gathered at George Washington Park, above, and slept where and when they could.

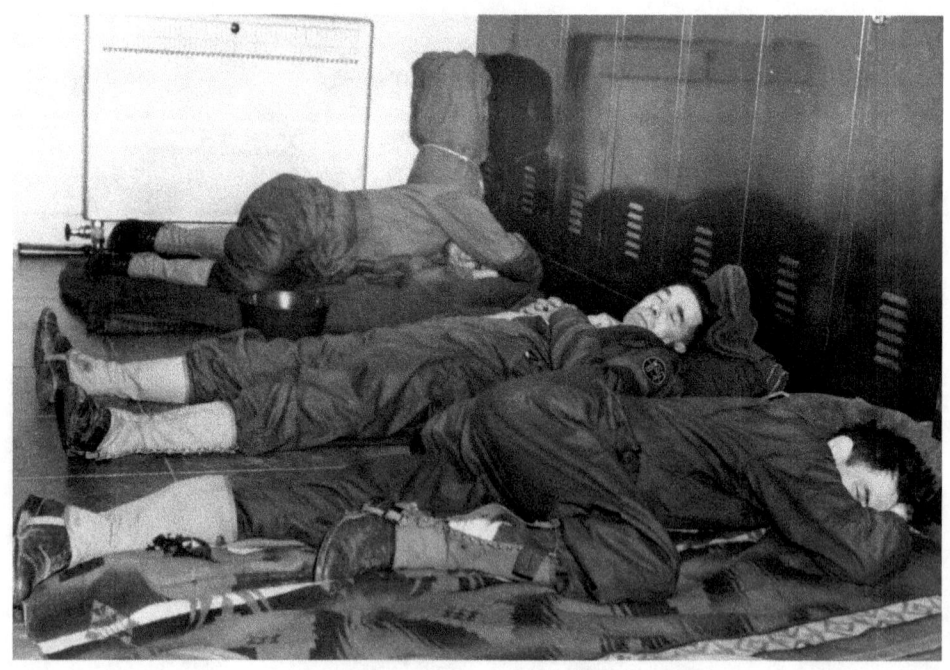

LEWIS COUNTY HISTORICAL MUSEUM P3651

LEWIS COUNTY HISTORICAL MUSEUM P15763

LEWIS COUNTY HISTORICAL MUSEUM P20112

A happy occasion on July 11, 1942, quickly turned sad when Florence Toothaker of Centralia celebrated her wedding, only to send her husband, Army Air Corps Lt. Louis Miller, off to war where he was killed in action in the South Pacific. At left, Centralia High girls sit on the front steps of the school in 1947. Below, the school is seen that same year.

LEWIS COUNTY HISTORICAL MUSEUM P20113

LEWIS COUNTY HISTORICAL MUSEUM P1189

LEWIS COUNTY HISTORICAL MUSEUM P9802

Lewis County Historical Museum P11886

A young man walks past the debris after Dr. Rice's damaged car was removed. At left, a young boy strides past the mess without looking at the earthquake-damaged building.

Lewis County Historical Museum P11888

LEWIS COUNTY HISTORICAL MUSEUM P11887

A man moves rock and debris to uncover Dr. Rice's car, above, and the damaged Matz building.

LEWIS COUNTY HISTORICAL MUSEUM P9705

Nine

Decades of Development

Frigid temperatures and a record snowstorm buried Centralia in early January 1950, with 17½ inches falling on January 13, when temperatures dropped to 15 degrees. Two days later, nearly twenty inches of snow covered the ground with twice that amount in snowdrifts from blowing snow. The January 1950 blizzard, dubbed the worst winter storm statewide in more than thirty-five years, closed schools, blocked highways, and forced businesses to shutter temporarily. The cold and snow continued off and on all month, culminating with record low temperatures of two degrees above zero officially recorded downtown on February 1st, 2nd, and 3rd.

And in warmer weather, the city of Centralia constructed an outdoor swimming pool in the 1950s to honor those who served during World War II and called it the Veterans Memorial Pearl Street Pool. With so many soldiers drowning on D-Day as they invaded the Normandy beaches, the citizens built the pool to teach young people at home how to swim. It operated for three decades until the city closed it in the early 1980s. Friends in Need, a local nonprofit, urged its reopening four years later, and operated it from 1984 until 2008, when the city resumed control of the pool. It closed the pool again in 2011, citing low attendance and increased maintenance and operating costs. For a decade, volunteers in the grassroots Save The Outdoor Pool (STOP) group struggled to raise money and fought to reopen the pool. STOP helped pay for construction of the $258,704 Pearl Street Memorial Plaza with the Pearl Street

Spray Park, which opened in the summer of 2017. But in February 2023, the council voted to close the pool permanently. The STOP group donated money raised to save the pool to local nonprofits.

The biggest change in the 1950s was construction of Interstate 5 along the West Coat of the United States, connecting California to the Canadian border. It bypassed the traditional north-south Pacific Highway formed in 1913 from wagon trails and military roads. It was paved in the 1920s, and the Peace Arch in Blaine at the Canadian border was dedicated on September 4, 1923. The Pacific Highway drew traffic through Centralia and Chehalis as well as other small towns along the route. Most of that highway was folded into Route 99, or U.S. Highway 99, in 1926. Planning for a federal superhighway system began in the late 1930s and Congress provided funding in 1944.

Construction began in Southwest Washington on what became Interstate 5 in late 1951, with a section near Kalama opening in 1952. The section through Centralia and Chehalis, completed in the mid-1950s, bypassed Tenino and other small towns. The government created the Interstate Highway System in 1957, with I-5 a component of it. Workers completed the final segment through Washington between Everett and Marysville on May 14, 1969.

Excitement heralded the whistlestop of General Dwight D. Eisenhower during his 1952 campaign for U.S. president when his train stopped for water at the Centralia depot on October 7. About four thousand people packed the station and a few perched on the roof to glimpse the man who helped America win World War II, a national hero seeking the highest office in the land. He stood at the back of a train car beside his wife, Mamie Eisenhower, and waved to the people gathered for a glimpse of the man who would become president. He signed autographs for children and chatted with people. He mentioned having stopped in Centralia in 1940 with the Army on maneuvers and tossed "Ike" rings and buttons to people.

Six local residents in September 1959 formed a charter committee responsible for the development of Evergreen Playhouse, a community theater where actors perform on a stage for an audience. Many of those involved in the creation of the playhouse were affiliated with Centralia College as instructors or trustees. They sold shares to finance the first production, Sabrina Fair, which debuted on January 14, 1960, in the ballroom of the Lewis and Clark Hotel. With donations from patrons, the group in 1972 bought the Church of the Open Bible on Center Street, which became the cozy community theater's home, Evergreen Playhouse.

Centralia and Chehalis city officials battled with residents to add fluoride to city water to cut down on dental decay. Downtown parking meters were removed in Centralia. The Centralia Police Department hired its first civilian dispatchers and clerical support to file records, freeing police officers to solve crimes. The department employed twenty-three officers in 1977, a number that dropped through attrition in the next decade.

In 1956, Centralia School District voters approved a $1.36 million bond and special levy for a school building modernization project. Centralia built a new $100,000 fire hall the same year.

The 1960s brought an escalation in the fighting in Southeast Asia. The draft sent young men to a place called Vietnam that few knew anything about. And in 1967, a Milwaukee freight train traveling through Centralia spilled its shipment of 200 tons of aerial bombs bound for Vietnam.

Closer to home, excitement arose when Century 21 brought the World's Fair to Seattle from April to October in 1962. A 180-foot aluminum tower with an astronaut in a capsule at the top rose above Centralia, courtesy of the Twin Cities Chamber of Commerce, which erected it as part of the Seattle World's Fair events.

On Columbus Day, October 12, 1962, devastating hurricane-force winds of up to 100 miles per hour, known as Typhoon Freda, tore through the Pacific Northwest, killing forty-six people and injuring hundreds more. It blew down as much as 15 billion board feet of timber and caused up to $280 million in damage throughout Washington, Oregon, and California, which equates to more than $5 billion in today's dollars.

At 8:28 a.m. on April 29, 1965, an earthquake measuring 6.7 hit the Puget Sound region, killed eight people, and caused $12.5 million to $28 million in damages, including a crack in the dome and supporting buttresses of the Washington State Capitol building.

Chehalis tribal member Hazel Pete, who raised thirteen children and was renowned for her basket-weaving skills, taught at Centralia College and created the Hazel Pete Institute of Chehalis Basketry in her home.

In 1968, Centralia implemented its one-way traffic downtown, which confused police officers and drivers. One woman stopped and the officer asked if she knew she was driving on a one-way street. She responded, "Sure I do. I'm only going one way."

While a ghost town replaced the mining community of Mendota, Pacific Power & Light Company announced plans in 1967 to construct a $200 million coal-fired steam-powered electric plant in the Big Hanaford Valley east of

Centralia. It opened in 1969. The company constructed two coal-fired units, both capable of producing about 700 megawatts, and started generating power in 1971. It created Skookumchuck Dam, an earthen dam on the Skookumchuck River upriver from the town of Bucoda, to store water for the power plant. TransAlta, a Canadian company based in Calgary, Alberta, bought the mine and power plant from Pacific Power and Light in 2000 for $554 million. Between 1971 and November 2006, miners extracted 160 million tons of coal from the surface mine at Centralia, all of which was burned by the power plant. It operated around the clock for years and employed 850.

The year 1973 saw the opening of a restaurant well-known by travelers along Interstate 5 who know the rooster crows when the doors open at Country Cousin on Harrison Avenue, home of the old-fashioned pot roast. The menu has told the story of a time "when the world was flat and Centralia was the center of the known world."

Gas shortages topped headlines in 1974 as the energy crisis hit home. With rainfall down 30 percent, hydroelectric reservoir levels plummeted, creating a power crunch.

Although the Grace Seminary never opened as a normal school, the land surrounding the iconic building served as an outdoor classroom for hundreds of girls and boys who participated in day camps offered through the Scouts in the 1960s and 1970s. On April 2, 1980, a nonprofit group called The Friends of the Seminary Hill Natural Area formed. City officials decided to preserve seventy wooded acres once known as Centralia's Dry Park, a buffer around its water reservoirs, as the Seminary Hill Natural Area on March 17, 1981.

The Centralia Christian School opened in Centralia in 1979, sponsored by the Centralia First Christian Church, which created an addition to accommodate the school. But as enrollment increased, the school outgrew the building. Classes were held in several Protestant churches throughout the city until 1998, when the school purchased the Harland Company property at 1315 South Tower Avenue and renovated it.

In the late 1970s, Centralia became renowned in the Pacific Northwest as a hub for antique shops, starting with a few and expanding to host more than 350 dealers in two dozen or more shops along Pearl Street and Tower Avenue. The Centralia Square Antique Mall in the old Elks Lodge on Pearl Street also houses Berry Fields Café. Tower Avenue boasts Catty Wampus, Timeless Treasures, and Up the Creek Antiques, established in 1978.

Two prisoners of war in the Vietnam conflict—Air Force Major Edward W. Leonard of Winlock and Samuel Mattix, a Christian missionary from Centralia who was captured in Laos and held prisoner for five months—returned home to great fanfare in 1974. Three children died in a Centralia storage shed fire that critically burned a fourth.

Just as in earlier decades, China Creek flooded city streets during heavy rainfall in the 1950s, prompting some residents to travel by boat, and overflowing rivers sent water into homes and businesses. In November 1959, a king-sized logjam on the swollen Chehalis River butted up against the new Mellen Street bridge, and although pilings groaned and tilted under the stress, the span remained intact. Flooding in January 1965 that brought fatal mudslides and a flash flood to Randle in East Lewis County inundated Fords Prairie residents near Centralia and closed roads. The storm caused $430 million in damage throughout the Pacific Northwest.

In 1970, the earthen Skookumchuck Dam built to supply water to the steam-electric plant in the Hanaford Valley helped prevent flooding in western Lewis County by holding back three inches of rain. Flooding occurred again in January 1971, and the following year, in January 1972, the Chehalis River crested at Centralia at an all-time high (then), forcing residents of Long Road in Centralia to evacuate their homes and leaving parts of western Lewis County a sea of water. Water closed Harrison Avenue and North Pearl Street, covered portions of Interstate 5, and again flooded the Riverside Motel. Two feet of water filled the Yard Birds Shopping Center, and the Southwest Washington Fairgrounds flooded. Early estimates put damages to roads, buildings, and bridges at up to $5 million. Two years later, flooding occurred twice in January 1974, causing an estimated $10 million in damage. In December 1975, the Skookumchuck and Chehalis Rivers overflowed, flooding roads and forcing evacuation of the Chehalis Apartments. Local flooding occurred again in the Twin Cities, with two feet of water covering Kresky Avenue, in December 1977.

LEWIS COUNTY HISTORICAL MUSEUM P11119

The decade began with a frigid snowstorm in January 1950. The photo shows Main and Tower covered in snow. Below is a 1950 photo of a covered railroad bridge across the Chehalis River, near Galvin and Lincoln Creek.

LEWIS COUNTY HISTORICAL MUSEUM P17585

LEWIS COUNTY HISTORICAL MUSEUM P7859

The city opened the Veterans Memorial Pearl Street Pool in the early 1950s to teach children how to swim after so many soldiers drowned on D-Day in June 1944 while storming the beaches of Normandy because they didn't know how to swim. When the pool opened, it drew large crowds, especially on hot, summer days as seen in the photo below.

PHOTO COURTESY OF DAN DUFFY

LEWIS COUNTY HISTORICAL MUSEUM P9470

An aerial photo shows the route of Interstate 5 through the Twin Cities area during its construction in the early 1950s. The photo looks north, just west of Chehalis. Below is an undated photo of a bridge over the Skookumchuck being built as part of the Interstate 5 project.

LEWIS COUNTY HISTORICAL MUSEUM P11102

LEWIS COUNTY HISTORICAL MUSEUM P11103

Above, an undated photo shows a bridge under constructions as part of the Interstate 5 project. The Skookumchuck would later be diverted to run beneath the bridge. At right is a photo from July 1951 of Centralia Police Officer George Waterman.

LEWIS COUNTY HISTORICAL MUSEUM P15077

General Dwight D. Eisenhower, while campaign-ing for US president, made a 'whistle stop' at Centralia. Crowds gathered at the Centraila depot to await the moment his train stopped for water on October 7, 1952. In November he wont the election.

PHOTOS COURTESY OF *THE CHRONICLE*

LEWIS COUNTY HISTORICAL MUSEUM PC2418

These photos were both taken in about 1956. The top one shows Main Street and Tower Avenue, looking north on Tower. The lower photo shows Pine Street and North Tower Avenue, looking north on Tower.

LEWIS COUNTY HISTORICAL MUSEUM PC2345

A birds-eye view of Centralia in 1955 shows Interstate 5, the sewage treatment plant, Seminary Hill, the Fox Theatre, the Lewis Clark Hotel, Cardinal Door Factory, Centralia General Hospital, the Catholic School and Church, and the Standard Oil Bulk Plant.

Lewis County Historical Museum P14402

Abbot Townsend, age eighty-six, with his corn crop. The Daily Chronicle *noted Townsend as one of Centralia's "finest gardeners." He gave much of the produce from his gardens and fruit trees to neighbors and friends and family.*

PHOTO COURTESY OF ISAAC HARJO

Abbot Townsend of Centralia plants his garden at eighty-nine. He told The Daily Chronicle *that the secret to a long life is, "Do lots of hard work and let the other fellows drink the whiskey and smoke the cigarettes." He remembered much of life in Centralia from the early days, including the names of the thirteen original families and the location of their homes. A year later, Townsend, then ninety in 1958, stands in front of the house on Yew Street he purchased from George Washington. A friend of Washington's, Townsend platted part of Centerville, naming its streets and creating lots. Townsend leans on a ladder he built himself so he could continue to prune trees and harvest the fruit. Townsend passed away the year this photo was taken. He lived in Centralia for seventy-nine years.*

PHOTOS COURTESY OF ISAAC HARJO

AUTHOR PHOTO

Citizens interested in community theater, including instructors at Centralia Junior College, established the Evergreen Playhouse in 1959, and the nonprofit has continued to entertain the community since then. The first play performed was 'Sabrina Fair.' In 1972, Evergreen Playhouse purchased a building at 226 West Center Street in Centralia. Below is the Centralia Space Needle erected in 1962 in honor of the World's Fair in Seattle. It was near Interstate 5 and Walt's Drive-In Restaurant.

LEWIS COUNTY HISTORICAL MUSEUM P18447

A closer photo of the Centralia Space Needle, at right. Below, eighteen-year-old Loren Wolff, "astronaut" for the Harrison Avenue Space Tower, who spent sixty days in the capsule at the top working with his radio set and speaking by phone to tourists who came to see the exhibit.

LEWIS COUNTY HISTORICAL MUSEUM P18450

LEWIS COUNTY HISTORICAL MUSEUM P14627

LEWIS COUNTY HISTORICAL MUSEUM P8685

The October 12, 1962, Columbus Day storm damaged homes, cars, and airplances. The Centralia Fire Department staff, below. Names are on the next page.

LEWIS COUNTY HISTORICAL MUSEUM P20927

LEWIS COUNTY HISTORICAL MUSEUM P7837

Above is a photo of Ken Schoenfeld Furniture taken in 1969 or 1970. Before this, the building was home to a bank and the Elks Club. Later it became an antique mall. At left, members of the Centralia Fire Department stand in front of a truck and the station on November 22, 1976. From left are Chief Richard Lee, LaRue Breckenridge, Dana Williams, Larry Hall, Lloyd Zadina, Mark Herniston, and Robert Shirer.

The Chehalis River Valley has flooded for decades. This photo shows flooding in 1973.

The Centralia Church of the Nazarene completed its building on West First Street in Centralia in the early 1960s.

LEWIS COUNTY HISTORICAL MUSEUM P12415

LEWIS COUNTY HISTORICAL MUSEUM P20255

In the early 1970s, the Church of Jesus Christ of Latter-Day Saints erected this building at 2801 Mount Vista Road west of Fort Borst Park.

LEWIS COUNTY HISTORICAL MUSEUM P12407

LEWIS COUNTY HISTORICAL MUSEUM P2632

By the 1970s, old buildings were being repurposed. This 1974 photo shows the Tribune Printing Company in Centralia using a building constructed in 1912 as the Farmers and Merchant Bank. It was owned by C. Paul Uhlmann. The bank used the main floor of the building and rented the upstairs for offices. By 1936, the building housed Yeager's Bakery, which sold cheese bread, pastries, and cakes, among other baked goods. The building today houses the Hub City Honey Company.

Ten

Dawn of a New Millennium

During the late 1970s and early 1980s, the commercial landscape of the Hub City changed dramatically, shifting from a forest-based economy to one dependent on retail. It started with closure of forestland to protect the northern spotted owl, prompting logging operations and sawmills to lay off workers. The Washington Public Power Supply System defaulted on its bonds in 1983, issued to build a nuclear plant at Satsop. The economy dove into a recession.

But then John Regan brought a new vision to the city when he opened the Centralia Square Antique Mall in the old Elks Lodge on Pearl Street in 1986. He later worked with realtor Dean Proffitt to purchase land off Interstate 5 near Exit 82 and invested $5 million to develop the Centralia Outlets, which opened in February 1988 with its first tenant, London Fog. Six more stores soon joined in the Northwest's first outlet center, bringing hope to a struggling city seeking businesses and jobs. The outlets, which underwent major renovation in March 2006, employ nearly three hundred people and remain a huge attraction drawing visitors to Centralia.

The structure of Centralia's city government also changed in 1986 when voters approved changing from a three-commissioner form of government to one governed by a paid city manager and seven unpaid Centralia City Council members. City voters had adopted the commission form of government in 1911, with a full-time paid mayor and two full-time commissioners overseeing all departments. An effort by local business leaders in 1932 to abolish the commission failed, but a half century later, a similar attempt succeeded. The council elected

Lee Coumbs, a former Southwest Washington Fair manager and schoolteacher, as the first mayor. The council hired Pat Scheidel of Narragansett, Rhode Island, as the city's first city manager.

With students taught in a relatively new $2.7 million Centralia High School, which opened on September 2, 1969, the future looked brighter. Centralia College demolished the old Lincoln Grade School to construct a new fine arts building, Corbet Hall. In 1970, the Centralia School District built a new Tiger Stadium on the south side of the high school track. In the late 1970s, the district remodeled Washington and Oakview schools while the old Jefferson Grade School building and later the old Roosevelt building were demolished.

In 1980, the school district paired with the city's Parks and Recreation Department to construct a new indoor swimming pool near the district office on Johnson Road. The new Centralia-Chehalis Pupil Transportation Cooperative started in the spring of 1982, providing buses for students in both districts. By the mid-1980s, computers were in nearly every classroom. More classrooms were added to Fords Prairie in 1984, and in 1985, Harry Pratley donated to Fords Prairie the original bell that rang in the school during the late 1800s. In 1986, the district added four portable classrooms behind Centralia High School. Modernization and expansion of the Centralia Junior High began in 1987, and in September that year, middle school students were moved to the new Centralia Middle School. Remodeling of Edison Elementary was completed by September 1988. The district sold the old Galvin School for $30,000 in March 1989. In 1991, the district sought voter approval for its first two-year maintenance and operations levy but postponed proposing a bond to modernize schools because of the uncertain economy. In 1993, the district asked voters to approve a $10.5 million bond to modernize schools, but it was defeated. Voters also rejected a $5 million bond for remodeling proposed in May 1995.

The Pacific Northwest gained national attention in 1980 when Mount St. Helens erupted on May 18, killing fifty-seven people and causing billions of dollars in damages.

Only a few months later, Centralia launched Summerfest, a free family-oriented Fourth of July event complete with a parade, pancake breakfast, games and competitions, fishing derby, and an afternoon barbecue at Fort Borst Park. The historic Borst home is open for tours as are the one-room schoolhouse and pioneer church. Summerfest often includes a public fireworks display at the Southwest Washington Fairgrounds.

In 1982, citizens remodeled the Fox Theatre, but it closed again in 1998. The city bought the building in 2007, and a nonprofit formed to raise about $5 million needed to restore the historic theater. In 2003, the city sold the Fox Theatre to Opera Pacifica.

Also in the early 1980s, Richard Tracy, a department manager and janitor at the Yard Birds Mall in Chehalis for thirty years, began erecting Styrofoam sculptures in black, white, and gray in the large yard surrounding his home in Centralia. Among his creations was an eight-foot-tall, 450-pound Yard Bird. A 2001 film called "Richart" featured his yard, which entertained and enticed passersby, including the McMenamin brothers, who left the freeway in 1996 to see the unusual artistic display and later bought and restored the historic Olympic Club.

The city's police department implemented a 911 system in 1979 and operated it until Chehalis began dispatching for both cities in 1984. Then the county implemented an enhanced 911 service central dispatch center in 1995. The city had closed its jail a decade earlier, opting to use Chehalis and Lewis County facilities instead. By 1996, the police department had thirty commissioned officers.

State lawmakers passed legislation in 1986 that opened the door for the creation of inland port districts, and voters on September 16 of that year approved creation of the Port of Centralia.

They elected three commissioners to oversee the new district, which levied a tax and began purchasing property in the Galvin Road area in 1990. Roger's Machinery became the first tenant in 1994, followed by other companies such as Simpson Door Company, Michael's Distribution Center, Centralia Sawmill, Scot Industries, Mowat Construction, Opus Northwest, Dick's Brewing, STIHL Northwest, United Natural Foods Inc., and Gorham Printing, a commercial printing company that started in 1976 and relocated from south Thurston County. The port constructed administrative offices near the turn of the century and worked with city and county officials to develop roads in the port's new industrial park. In 2013, the port announced development of the forty-three-acre Centralia Station, which included an unnamed anchor store, eventually WinCo in 2025. The port worked with state transportation officials to develop freeway access to the property. Centralia Station, with its ten stores, four restaurants, bank, and gas station is expected to employ nearly seven hundred people and boost the local economy by $118 million a year.

In 1985, eleven years after starting a practice in Centralia, ophthalmologist Dr. Helgi Heidar, an Iceland native who pioneered LASIK (laser-assisted in situ keratomileusis) eye surgery techniques, cofounded the Pacific Cataract and Laser Institute in Chehalis with Dr. Robert Ford. The company, which has expanded throughout Washington, Oregon, Idaho, Montana, and Alaska, has performed nearly a million micro eye surgeries.

The 1980s brought only one major flood, in November 1986, when China Creek, swollen by heavy rainfall, overflowed through downtown Centralia. Floodwaters inundated homes, businesses, and Washington Elementary School, sweeping mud and debris into classrooms and hallways. The school had to be evacuated and closed for three days so staff could clean and sanitize everything. High water left motorists stranded and, in Chehalis, spread a toxic wood treatment chemical called pentachlorophenol through a residential neighborhood of about two hundred homes. Three feet of water covered Kresky Avenue, ten feet filled buildings at the Southwest Washington Fairgrounds after a dike broke, and traffic on Interstate 5 was limited to one lane.

During the 1990s, Lewis County experienced two five-hundred-year floods within six years. Two people died during flooding in January 1990 when they tried to escape after water swamped their vehicles, one on the freeway near Chehalis and another near the Skookumchuck River on Waunch Prairie. Lowland flooding occurred again in February 1990 and again in November 1990 during a storm that the National Weather Service rated as Washington's tenth major weather event of the century behind the 1962 Columbus Day Storm, the January 1950 blizzard with record cold and snowfall, massive forest fires in 1910, and the 1980 eruption of Mount St. Helens.

Six years later, in February 1996, Lewis County experienced what the National Weather Service ranked No. 8 on a list of Washington's most significant weather events of the 20th century. Heavy rain and rising freezing levels filled the Chehalis and Skookumchuck Rivers, which both crested at their highest levels ever (until December 2007). Schools and businesses shut down, roads closed and floodwaters from the Chehalis once again closed Interstate 5 between Centralia and Chehalis, with water more than six feet deep over the freeway. The floodwater damaged homes, schools and churches throughout Centralia and throughout the region. Afterward, Centralia city officials recommended all new buildings be raised a foot above the 1996 flood level. Statewide, the flood killed three and caused $800 million in damages.

A highlight for Centralia residents occurred on September 19, 1996, when 18,000 people packed the corner of Tower Avenue and Pine Street downtown to see US President Bill Clinton and Vice President Al Gore and their wives during their Building a Bridge to the 21st Century re-election campaign tour. A dozen years later, a much smaller crowd of fifty gathered for the dedication of a bronze plaque in a monument marking their visit to Centralia.

That's also the year the McMenamin brothers bought and restored the historic Olympic Club in 1996 after stopping to see Richard Tracy's art yard.

A man who heard God call him in the middle of the night in 1994 set out to ensure that the sacrifices of veterans who served this country would be honored and remembered. To that end, Lee Grimes recorded veterans' stories, collected memorabilia, and opened a museum in Centralia after mortgaging his home to pay for remodeling the old War-Mur Electric & Telephone building at 712 W. Main Street. The museum opened on Veterans Day, November 11, 1997, to great fanfare. It continued to thrive and, outgrowing its location, constructed the 22,000-square-foot Veterans Memorial Museum off Interstate 5's Exit 77 in Chehalis, which opened in 2005. Bronze lettering on the side of the building states the museum's mission: "They Shall Not Be Forgotten."

In the mid-1990s, Scottish Power paid $7.5 billion for PacifiCorp, owners of the Centralia steam-electric plant, then sold both the mine and the plant in 1999 to TransAlta, a Canadian company, for $554 million. At the time, the plant employed 670 workers with an annual payroll of $37 million.

The new millennium in Centralia brought both hope and sorrow to its residents. The hype over Y2K, with doom-and-gloom predictions of computers crashing and the end of the world looming, proved to be just that—hype. Life continued as usual.

On February 8, 2001, a 6.8-magnitude earthquake centered at McNeil Island broke a waterline and flooded several rooms at Jefferson Lincoln Elementary School. The following year, a portable room at the school was destroyed in a fire caused by a faulty heating unit. Also in 2002, local artists decided to highlight their work and their studios to the public through formation of ARTrails of Southwest Washington, held the third and fourth weekends of September to let people watch as many as sixty local artists display their creations.

For three years in a row, from 2003 to 2005, bond proposals for Centralia school remodels failed to reach a 60 percent supermajority. The war in the Middle East hit home especially in 2005 with the death of local resident Regina Clark, a Navy reserve petty officer who had worked at Fuller's Market Basket in Centralia, during Operation Iraqi Freedom.

Finally, in 2006, 65 percent of voters supported a new school levy. For the next decade, all but one school levy passed. A devastating fire at Oakview Elementary in May destroyed one wing with ten classrooms and forced cancellation of school for nearly a week. On November 27, 2006, under increasing pressure over carbon and mercury emissions, TransAlta closed its open-pit coal mine, the last commercial coal mine in Washington, and laid off 600 workers. Construction to rebuild at Oakview Elementary School began on September 7, 2007. On December 3, 2007, a devastating flood inundated twenty blocks near downtown Centralia as well as residential neighborhoods, covering a twenty-mile stretch of Interstate 5, closing the freeway for several days. Eight people died throughout the region and damage totaled billions of dollars.

In 2003, downtown Centralia won recognition on the National Register of Historic Place.

On January 1, 2008, the Centralia Fire Department joined Lewis County Fire District No. 12 under leadership of the newly formed Riverside Fire Authority. In February, a replacement levy passed, and the new Oakview Elementary School wing opened in October. In early January 2009, heavy rains once again caused flooding. In June, TransAlta donated money for a new track at Centralia High School. The city, school district, TransAlta, and Lewis County Public Facilities District donated money to build a new sports complex in Tiger Stadium, dedicated on October 8, 2010.

In 2013, the Port of Centralia announced development of the forty-three-acre Centralia Station, which includes WinCo Foods as an anchor store, and worked with state transportation officials to develop freeway access to the property. In September 2014, the indoor Northwest Sports Hub, built on Centralia School District land near Fort Borst Park, opened to the public. A year later, city officials estimated it brought in $4.2 million in local revenue and $1.9 million to local hotels. The following year, in 2015, brought more flood concerns when the Chehalis, Newaukum, and Skookumchuck Rivers threatened to overflow their banks in early January. While major damage was avoided, government officials with the Chehalis River Basin Flood Authority continued to study possible flood prevention options. Centralia received state funding to create more water storage on donated land to curtail flooding of China Creek.

The $128 million I-5 Mellen to Blakeslee Junction highway project, completed in 2016, was designed to reduce congestion and improve safety. In February 2017, Centralia voters approved a $74 million bond, the largest in the district's history, to modernize the high school and build new schools at Fords Prairie and Jefferson Lincoln. Construction of the new schools began in 2019, marking the first new schools built in Centralia in half a century. The old schools were torn down that year. By 2020, the city of Centralia had 18,183 residents, with the population continuing to grow.

Today, TransAlta employs fewer than a hundred people in Centralia. National Public Radio in 2024 featured TransAlta and Centralia, a city of nearly 19,000 residents, as an example of the right way to phase out a coal-fired power plant, which is slated to shut down permanently by December 31, 2025. The plant developed a transitioning memorandum of agreement with the state in 2011. As it phased out the plant, the company provided $55 million in grants to support the community and has worked to reclaim the 8,600 acres mined for coal by planting trees.

Centralia Station, with its ten stores, four restaurants, bank, and gas station, is expected to employ over 500 people and boost the local economy by $118 million a year. Its anchor business, WinCo Foods, opened on April 7, 2025, twelve years after its announcement.

During the past 150 years, Centerville—Centralia—and its people have proven to be resilient, tenacious, and eager to grasp the realities facing them each day. Local officials look forward to a bright future, which is nearly guaranteed based on its rich past.

LEWIS COUNTY HISTORICAL MUSEUM PC2561

The postcard above shows Tower Avenue in Centralia in the 1980s, looking north from Main and Tower. At left is the Galvin Bible Chapel.

LEWIS COUNTY HISTORICAL MUSEUM P2724

LEWIS COUNTY HISTORICAL MUSEUM P17843

The First Assembly of God gathered for worship in 1987 at the historic building above on North Tower Avenue. The building formerly held the Liberty Theatre and a barber shop. Below is a photo of founding member Millard Seymore in front of Mountain View Baptist Church in Centralia.

LEWIS COUNTY HISTORICAL MUSEUM P10751

Centralia has remade its identity in the past forty years, creating a reputation for saving money at the Centralia Outlets and finding treasures at the antique shops.

AUTHOR PHOTOS

AUTHOR PHOTOS

Seminary Hill Natural Area at Locust Street and Barner Drive in Centralia serves as an outdoor classroom for people of all ages with free educational programs offered in the summertime. Trails let people enjoy nature and learn about geology, trees, plants, and wildlife. Below is a marker covering a time capsule buried during the city's 1886 centennial, celebrating the first one hundred years since its creation in 1886 by the Washington Territorial Legislature. It's set to be opened in 2036 on the city's 150th anniversary.

LEWIS COUNTY HISTORICAL MUSEUM P10639

Above is a photo of northwest Centralia during the January 1990 flooding caused by the overflowing of China Creek. Below is the home of Richard Tracy, who created Styrofoam sculptures in his three-lot yard at Harrison Avenue and M Street. He started building artistic creations on his property in the early 1980s and dismantled it before his death in December 2022.

AUTHOR PHOTO

AUTHOR PHOTO

It was Richard Tracy's unusual yard art that drew the McMenamin brothers off Interstate 5. They then drove through downtown Centralia and discovered the historic Olympic Club, which they restored into a restaurant, bar, and hotel complete with a theater.

PHOTOS COURTESY OF *THE CHRONICLE*

It was a red-letter day on September 19, 1996, when 18,000 people turned out to see US President Bill Clinton and Vice President Al Gore and their wives, Hillary Clinton and Tipper Gore, during their visit to Centralia. The Chronicle captured the excitement in a special section commemorating the event.

Tower Avenue in the new millennium.

AUTHOR PHOTOS

Bibliography

"Elkanah Mills." Find a Grave. Accessed July 25, 2025.
 https://www.findagrave.com/memorial/20863543/elkanah-mills.
"Eva Estella Borst McElfresh." Find a Grave. Accessed July 25, 2025.
 https://www.findagrave.com/memorial/102691350/eva_estella-mcelfresh.
"Francis Marian 'Frank' Waunch." Find a Grave. Accessed July 25, 2025.
 https://www.findagrave.com/memorial/20864218/francis-marian-waunch.
"George Leonard Waunch Jr." Find a Grave. Accessed July 25, 2025.
 https://www.findagrave.com/memorial/13341941/george_leonard-waunch.
"Honoring Our Elders: Curtis Levi Dupuis, Sr." *Chehalis Tribal Newsletter*. Sept. 2009, Vol. 2/9. https://www.chehalistribe.org/newsletter/archives/2009-09/mobile/index.html#p=1.
In the Service: The Great World War Honor Roll Southwest Washington. Centralia, WA: F. H. Cole Printing Co, n.d.
"Jessie Ford Elam." Find a Grave. Accessed July 25, 2025.
 https://www.findagrave.com/memorial/57025474/jessie-elam.
"Mary Adeline Roundtree Borst." Find a Grave. Accessed July 25, 2025.
 https://www.findagrave.com/memorial/24973918/mary_adeline-borst.
"Skoukuma John 'Plug-Ugly' Youckton." Find a Grave. Accessed July 25, 2025.
 https://www.findagrave.com/memorial/104579881/skoukuma-john-youckton#viewphoto=170029434.
Access Genealogy. "History of Centralia, Washington." Accessed July 29, 2025.
 https://accessgenealogy.com/washington/history-of-centralia-washington.htm.
Alzatraz History. "Roy Gardner." OceanView Publishing. Accessed July 30, 2025.
 https://www.alcatrazhistory.com/gardner.htm.
American Red Cross. "Women an Important Part of American Red Cross History." Feb. 28, 2023. https://www.redcross.org/about-us/news-and-events/news/2023/women-an-important-part-of-red-cross-history.html#:~:text=AMERICAN%20RED%20CROSS%20CANTEEN%20SERVICE,Cross%20during%20World%20War%20I.
Banel, Feliks. "Cowlitz Convention Responsible for Splitting Washington from Oregon." *MyNorthwest* (Seattle, WA), Aug. 29, 2017.
Centralia School District No. 401, "History of Centralia Schools,"
 https://www.centraliaschooldistrict.org/apps/pages/index.jsp?uREC_ID=3715672&type=d&pREC_ID=2427241.
Centralia College and *The Chronicle*, "A Timeline: 90 Years of Education at Centralia College," December 25, 2015.
Chehalis Bee Nugget. (Centralia, WA), July 27, 1900.

Ciranny Zopolos, Sarah. *Laboring in Love: Angelo and Teresa Ciranny: From Italy to Tono to Centralia*. Chapters of Life, Jan. 1, 2007.

Citizens of Centralia. *Centralia's First Century 1845 – 1955*, Bicentennial ed. Tumwater, WA: H. J. Quality Printing, 1977.

City of Centralia. "Fort Borst Park." Accessed July 25, 2025. https://www.cityofcentralia.com/Facilities/Facility/Details/Fort-Borst-Park-39.

City of Centralia. "George Washington Park." Accessed July 26, 2025. https://cityofcentralia.com/Facilities/Facility/Details/George-Washington-Park-11.

City of Centralia. "Greenwood Cemetery Burials." Aug. 8, 2024. https://www.cityofcentralia.com/DocumentCenter/View/3636/Greenwood-Cemetery-Burials-as-of-August-8-2024.

City of Cosmopolis. "Cosmopolis History." Accessed July 15, 2025. https://www.cosmopoliswa.gov/community-resources/economic-development/history.html.

Cunningham, Curt. "History of Centralia." The Historic Pacific Highway in Washington. Accessed July 29, 2025. https://www.pacific-hwy.net/centralia1.htm.

Flora, Stephanie. "Emigrants to Oregon in 1845." Oregon Pioneers. Accessed July 29, 2025. http://www.oregonpioneers.com/1845.htm.

Fund, Edna. "Today in History: 'Fast Cat' Survives Freeway Trip in 1961." *The Chronicle* (Centralia, WA), Nov. 15, 2011. https://www.chronline.com/stories/today-in-history-fast-cat-survives-freeway-trip-in-1961,152987.

Fund, Edna. "Today in History: Building of Farmers and Merchants Bank Begins in 1911." *The Chronicle* (Centralia, WA), Mar. 30, 2011. https://www.chronline.com/stories/today-in-history-building-of-farmers-and-merchants-bank-begins-in-1911,166801.

George Washington Bicentennial and Beyond. "Bicentennial Celebration & Statue Dedication." Accessed July 29, 2025. https://ourgeorgewashington.com/about-us/bicentennial-celebration-statue-dedication/.

Governor's Office of Indian Affairs. "Quinault Treaty, 1856." Accessed July 14, 2025. https://goia.wa.gov/resources/treaties/quinault-treaty-1856.

Governor's Office of Indian Affairs. "Treaty of Medicine Creek, 1854." Accessed July 14, 2025. https://goia.wa.gov/resources/treaties/treaty-medicine-creek-1854.

Griswold, Marie, and Fred Shortman. "Honoring Our Elders: Marie Griswold." Chehalis Tribal Tribune. Feb. 2009, Vol. 2/2. https://www.chehalistribe.org/newsletter/archives/2009-02/mobile/index.html#p=3.

Hatch, Addy. "Black History in the Northwest." *Washington State Magazine*, Spring 2024. https://magazine.wsu.edu/2024/02/01/black-history-in-the-northwest/.

Hub City Honey. "Nature's Sweet Symphony: Discover the Essence of Raw Honey." Accessed July 26, 2025. https://hubcityhoneyco.com/.

Johnson, Karen. "Centralia, Washington (1875 -)." BlackPast. Jan. 19, 2007. https://www.blackpast.org/african-american-history/centralia-washington/.

Jones, Pat. "Plenty Still to Learn from Pioneer Woman." *The Chronicle* (Centralia, WA), June 10, 2006.

Krohn, Elise. "Camas." Washington Office of Superintendent of Public Instruction. Accessed July 24, 2025.

Lewis County Genealogical Society. "Mother of All Counties." Accessed July 29, 2025. https://www.walcgs.org/history.html.

Lewis County Historical Museum Photo Archive. https://lewiscountymuseum.org/photos/.

Lincoln Creek Lumber. "Family Owned for Five Generations." Accessed July 26, 2025. https://www.lincolncreeklumber.com/about-us.

McDonald Zander, Julie. "Native American Women: Rooted in the Land." PowerPoint presentation to the St. Helens Club, Centralia, WA, Sept. 2023.

McDonald Zander, Julie. *Bucoda: The Little Town with a Million Memories.* Chapters of Life, 2010.

McDonald Zander, Julie. Centralia College: Its People and Their Stories. Chapters of Life, 2016.

McDonald Zander, Julie. *Washington Territory's Grand Lady: The Story of Matilda (Glover) Koontz Jackson.* Chapters of Life Memory Books, Oct. 26, 2019.

McDonald, Julie. "Cowlitz Convention Laid Groundwork for Creating Washington State." *The Chronicle* (Centralia, WA), Aug. 29, 2017.

McDonald, Julie. "First U.S. Flag Flew in Lewis County July 4, 1853." *The Chronicle* (Centralia, WA), July 3, 2018.

McDonald, Julie. "Mills Legacy Preserved in Rochester Greenbelt." *The Chronicle* (Centralia, WA), Oct. 11, 2022.

McDonald, Julie. "Nancy Ford Descendant Shares Living History Free in One-Woman Play." *The Chronicle* (Centralia, WA), Oct. 29, 2019.

McDonald, Julie. "Pioneer Edward Warbass Jumped Toledo Claim of Simon Plamondon Jr." *The Chronicle* (Centralia, WA), Apr. 26, 2022.

McDonald, Julie. "Tenino Native with Pioneer Roots Celebrates 105th Birthday This Month." *The Chronicle* (Centralia, WA), Jan. 7, 2020.

McDonald, Julie. "Visit the Borst Home Saturday to Glimpse Life in the 1800s." *The Chronicle* (Centralia, WA), Oct. 4, 2016.

McDonald, Julie. "White Settlers Flee to Blockhouses During Indian Wars." *The Chronicle* (Centralia, WA), Sept. 27, 2022.

McMenamins Blog History Department. "George Washington: African American Pioneer and Founder of Centralia." McMenamins Blog. Feb. 2, 2023. https://blog.mcmenamins.com/george-washington-african-american-pioneer-and-founder-of-centralia/.

Mittge, Brian, and Kerry MacGregor Serl. *George Washington of Centralia: How the Pioneering Son of a Slave Crossed the Continent, Founded a Town, and Saved It During Its Darkest Hours.* Peace and Plenty Press, 2018.

National Archives and Records Administration. "The Deadly Virus: The Influenza Epidemic of 1918." Accessed July 29, 2025. https://www.archives.gov/exhibits/influenza-epidemic/.

National Society Daughters of the American Colonists. "Military Road, Washington Territory." Accessed July 17, 2025. https://nsdac.org/work-of-the-society/historical/markers/military-road-washington-territory/.

Oldham, Kit. "Bush, George (1790? – 1863)." HistoryLink. Jan. 31, 2004. https://www.historylink.org/file/5645.

Oldham, Kit. "George and Mary Jane Washington Found the Town of Centerville (now Centralia) on January 8, 1875." HistoryLink. Feb. 23, 2003.

Oregon Secretary of State. "Steam Donkeys and Lumberjack Food." Accessed July 26, 2025. https://sos.oregon.gov/archives/exhibits/ghost/Pages/logging-steam.aspx.

Ott, Jennifer. "Centralia—Thumbnail History." HistoryLink. Feb. 12, 2008. https://www.historylink.org/file/8487.

Ott, Jennifer. "George Waunch Files a Claim Near Future Centralia on Land That Will Become Known as Waunch Prairie on October 26, 1853." HistoryLink. May 8, 2008. https://www.historylink.org/File/8505.

Ott, Jennifer. "Looking Back on 150 Years of History for the City of Centralia." *The Chronicle* (Centralia, WA), Jan. 10, 2025. https://www.chronline.com/stories/looking-back-on-150-years-of-history-for-the-city-of-centralia,373413.

"Parade of headlines for decade of 60s," *The Daily Chronicle*, January 3, 1970.

Pearson, Adam, "Historic Downtown Centralia Building Burns." *The Chronicle* (Centralia, WA), Feb. 14, 2012. https://www.chronline.com/stories/historic-downtown-centralia-building-burns,145750.

Planes of Fame Air Museum. "Curtiss Robin J-1." Accessed July 26, 2025. https://planesoffame.org/aircraft/J-1.

Pucci, Carol. "Used to Hard Times, Centralia Happy to Show Its Proud Past." *The Spokesman-Review* (Spokane, WA), Oct. 24, 2010. http://spokesman.com/stories/2010/oct/24/seasoned-centralia/.

Rabbeson, Antonio B. "The Pioneer of '46. His Interesting Reminiscences of the First American Settlements…" *The Tacoma Ledger* (Tacoma, WA), May 9, 1886.

Revisiting Washington. "Centralia." Accessed July 30, 2025. https://revisitwa.org/waypoint/centralia/.

Reynolds, Vera T. "Society Happenings." The Daily Hub (Centralia, WA), Apr. 13, 1916. https://washingtondigitalnewspapers.org/?a=d&d=DH19160413.2.30&e=-------en-20--1--txt-txIN-------.

Schwartz, Eric. "Centralia Erects Monument to Note Clintons' '96 Campaign Visit." *The Chronicle* (Centralia, WA), May 12, 2008.

Schwartz, Eric. "Remembering a Presidential Visit." *The Chronicle* (Centralia, WA), May 14, 2008.

Smith, Herndon. *Centralia: The First Fifty Years*. Centralia, WA: *The Daily Chronicle*, 1949.

Solomon, Molly. "200 Years Later, Centralia Celebrates Its Very Own George Washington." Oregon Public Broadcasting. Aug. 11, 2017. https://ourgeorgewashington.com/about-us/bicentennial-celebration-statue-dedication/.

Spitzer, Hugh D. "Pivoting to Progressivism: Justice Stephen J. Chadwick, the Washington Supreme Court, and Change in Early 20th-Century Judicial Reasoning and Rhetoric." *Pacific Northwest Quarterly* (Vol. 104, No. 3, pp. 107-21), Nov. 2014. https://ssrn.com/abstract=2423649.

The Agnew Company. "Company." Accessed July 26, 2025. https://theagnewcompany.com/company/.

The American Legion. "The Freedom Walk." Accessed July 26, 2025. https://www.legion.org/memorials/united-states/washington/united-states-washington-the-freedom-walk.

"2008: A Year Full of Lessons to Ponder." *The Chronicle* (Centralia, WA), Dec. 31, 2008.

"2016 Stories of the Year: A Final Look Back at the Big Headlines of the Past Year." *The Chronicle* (Centralia, WA), Jan. 3, 2017.

"Stories of the Year from the Greater Lewis County Area." *The Chronicle* (Centralia, WA), Jan. 1, 2016.

The Confederated Tribes of the Chehalis Reservation. "People of the Sands." Accessed July 24, 2025. https://www.chehalistribe.org/our-story/people-of-the-sands/.

The Cultural Landscape Foundation. "Centralia Downtown Historic District." Accessed July 29, 2025. https://www.tclf.org/centralia-downtown-historic-district.

The Editors of Encyclopaedia Britannica. "Centralia." Britannica. Accessed July 29, 2025. https://www.britannica.com/place/Centralia-Washington.

The History of Centralia. Community Development Program, 1955.

Thurston Regional Planning Council. "Confederated Tribes of the Chehalis Reservation: 2024 Statistical Profile." Dec. 2024.

"Top Stories," *The Daily Chronicle*, December, 28 1974

Vernon E. Jordan Law Library. "A Brief History of Civil Rights in the United States: The Reservation Era." Howard University School of Law. Accessed July 15, 2025. https://library.law.howard.edu/civilrightshistory/indigenous/reservation.

Washington State Arts Commission. "Hazel Pete." ArtsWA. Accessed July 24, 2025. https://www.arts.wa.gov/artist-collection/?request=record;id=4371;type=701.

Washington State History Museum. "Leschi: Justice in Our Time." Accessed July 14, 2025. https://web.archive.org/web/20071122040738/http:/washingtonhistoryonline.org/leschi/figures.htm.

Washington State Parks. "Jackson House State Park Heritage Site History." Accessed July 14, 2025. https://parks.wa.gov/about/news-center/field-guide-blog/jackson-house-state-park-heritage-site-history.

Wegley, Nancy A. "Legacy from the Past," March 30, 1984, Prepared by: Nancy A. Wigley, Community Relations Coordinator. Lewis County Historical Museum.

Wikipedia. "Centralia, Washington." Accessed July 29, 2025. https://en.wikipedia.org/wiki/Centralia,_Washington.

Wikipedia. "Oregon Missionaries." Accessed July 29, 2025. https://en.wikipedia.org/wiki/Oregon_missionaries.

Wilma, David. "Lewis County—Thumbnail History." HistoryLink. Sept. 1, 2005. https://www.historylink.org/file/7449/.

Wilma, David. "Michael T. Simmons Settles at Tumwater in October 1845." HistoryLink. Jan. 22, 2003. https://www.historylink.org/file/5089.

"Worst gas shortages just seen for early 1974." *The Daily Chronicle*, December 31 1973

Wright Blair, Kitty. Pioneer Musings. Chapters of Life, 2014.

Zander, Larry. "Borst Left Imprint on Centralia." *The Daily Chronicle* (Centralia, WA), Oct. 17, 1975.

Zylstra, Matthew. "A Look Back: Chamber Hosts Tour of Welfare Gardens Providing Food Assistance During the Great Depression." *The Chronicle* (Centralia, WA), June 17, 2022. https://www.chronline.com/stories/a-look-back-chamber-hosts-tour-of-welfare-gardens-providing-food-assistance-during-the-great,295563.

Zander, Julie McDonald. *Centralia College: Its People and Their Stories*. Chapters of Life. 2016.

About the Authors

JULIE McDONALD ZANDER, an award-winning journalist, earned a bachelor's degree in communications and political science from the University of Washington before working two decades as a newspaper reporter and editor. Through her personal history company, Chapters of Life, she has published more than seventy-five individual, family, and community histories. Both *Washington Territory's Grand Lady*,  her nonfiction book about Matilda Koontz Jackson, and her debut novel, *The Reluctant Pioneer*, were finalists for the Western Writers of America's Spur Award for Best Historical Novel and won Will Rogers Medallions. *Shattered Peace: A Century of Silence*, inspired by the Centralia Tragedy, is her second novel. She and her husband live in the Pacific Northwest, where they raised their two children.

NORA ZANDER grew up in Toledo, Washington, and remembers frequent trips to local Lewis County museums, history events, and libraries, where she watched her mother work tirelessly to support the preservation of local and personal histories. Inspired by both of her parents, who worked as editors and writers for *The Daily Chronicle* and other newspapers for decades, Nora earned a Certificate in Editing from the University of Washington, after obtaining her bachelor's degree in genetics and cell biology from Washington State University. Since then, she has worked as a freelance copyeditor, proofreader, and now, writer, including a publication in *Plant Methods*, a scientific journal, where she was listed as third author. She lives with her spouse and two cats in the Pacific Northwest.

www.ingramcontent.com/pod-product-compliance
Lightning Source LLC
Chambersburg PA
CBHW070642160426
43194CB00009B/1541